STARTER
Student's Book

in English

PETER VINEY
KAREN VINEY

OXFORD
UNIVERSITY PRESS

Great Clarendon Street, Oxford OX2 6DP

Oxford University Press is a department of the University of Oxford.
It furthers the University's objective of excellence in research,
scholarship, and education by publishing worldwide in

Oxford New York

Auckland Bangkok Buenos Aires Cape Town Chennai
Dar es Salaam Delhi Hong Kong Istanbul Karachi Kolkata
Kuala Lumpur Madrid Melbourne Mexico City Mumbai Nairobi
São Paulo Shanghai Taipei Tokyo Toronto

Oxford and Oxford English are registered trade marks of
Oxford University Press in the UK and in certain other countries

© Oxford University Press / Three Vee Limited 2002

The moral rights of the authors have been asserted

Database right Oxford University Press (maker)

First published 2002

No unauthorized photocopying

All rights reserved. No part of this publication may be reproduced,
stored in a retrieval system, or transmitted, in any form or by any
means, without the prior permission in writing of Oxford University
Press, or as expressly permitted by law, or under terms agreed
with the appropriate reprographics rights organization. Enquiries
concerning reproduction outside the scope of the above should
be sent to the ELT Rights Department, Oxford University Press,
at the address above

You must not circulate this book in any other binding or cover
and you must impose this same condition on any acquirer

ISBN 0 19 434050 3

Designed by Richard Morris, Stonesfield Design
Typeset in Meta
Printed in China

Contents

	UNIT TITLE	GRAMMAR	TOPICS
1	What's your name?	*be*: *is*, *What's your name?* *do*: *I don't know.* *my, your, his, her*	greetings names, A, B, C, D numbers 0–9
2	Are you a student?	*be*: singular: *am, is, are* *I, you, he, she* article: *a, Can you spell ...?*	alphabet jobs, titles spelling
3	Where are you from?	*be*, singular: *am, is, are* *Yes, it is.* / *No, it isn't.* article: *a / an*, *Where?*	countries, jobs nationalities names, e-mail
4	Hello, goodbye	*do /don't* in formulas *I don't understand.* *Do you speak ...?*	greetings, thanks asking for help languages, titles
5	What is it?	*be*: singular and plural *It is ...* / *They are ...* nouns, plurals, article: *a/an*	possessions numbers 10–20 identifying things
6	We're friends	*be*: plural, *are* *we, you, they are ...* *in, by*, adjectives	in a café *There you go.* *Anything (else)?*
7	Take out	*can*: *Can I have ...?* article: *the* linking: *and, or* *How much (is that)?*	minimal language fast food, prices numbers 30–90
8	What colour is it?	*be*: singular and plural: *It is ...* *They are ...* adjectives	describing things numbers 21–32 colours
9	This is your room ...	*be*: *There is ...* / *There are ...* *a, an, some, any* adjectives, *very*	hotels, rooms furniture numbers 21–99
10	Shopping	*How much is it?* / *are they?* *What size ...? Can I help you?* *I'm looking for ...*	minimal language shopping, clothes prices, sizes

Teacher's note: *For a full description of the contents, see the introduction to the Teacher's Book.*

CONTENTS

	UNIT TITLE	GRAMMAR	TOPICS
11	**What have you got?**	*have got*: singular, plural nouns: singular and plural *Who?*	possessions personal objects documents
12	**Families**	*have got*: singular, plural possessive *'s*: *Ann's book* *our, your, their*	families relations popular names
13	**Instructions**	base forms of verbs, imperatives *Listen, Don't talk, Be quiet.* *us, them*	instructions action verbs classroom verbs
14	**Where do you live?**	present simple: 1st, 2nd, 3rd person: *I live / She lives* *do, does*; prepositions *at, in, with*	home work education
15	**Times**	present simple: 3rd person *It opens ... / They close ...* *What time? When? on, at, from*	time (6.30, 6.45) places days of the week
16	**Asking for directions**	imperatives: *Go ..., turn (left)...* *Can you (help) me?* *I'm looking for ...*	directions, maps places, streets ordinal numbers
17	**Lifestyles**	present simple routines: *do, does* *have (lunch, a bath)* time expressions *at, in, on*	routines, work meals, breaks TV survey
18	**Flight to Orlando**	*would like* demonstratives: *this, that* uncountables with *'d like / have got*	requests, offers meals, courses menus
19	**What can you do?**	*can*: ability *I can swim. / I can't drive.* lexical verbs: *play, sing, swim* etc.	computers sports, leisure music
20	**Appointments**	*can*: requests, permission *can*: future request, *tomorrow* *How about ...? early, late, on time*	suggestions apologies months, dates
21	**What's she doing?**	present continuous: *is doing* reason: *Why? Because ...?* questions: *who, why, what, where*	action verbs describing activities answering phones

CONTENTS

	UNIT TITLE	GRAMMAR	TOPICS
22	**Plans**	present continuous for future plans future time words sympathetic listening	leisure holidays plans
23	**An evening out**	*do / does*: likes and dislikes *Let's ...* *How about? What about?*	suggestions making plans entertainment
24	**Likes and dislikes**	*do / does*: likes and dislikes *-ing* forms: *playing, doing* *Which?*	leisure activities going out / staying in sports, music
25	**What are you going to do?**	*going to* for future *What are you going to do?* *What's going to happen (next)?*	films life events
26	**Where was it?**	past simple: *was, were* past time words, *last ...* prepositions: *in, on, under*	talking about the past locations
27	**The weather**	past simple: *was / were* adjectives *What was it like? How was it?*	weather meeting strangers flights, holidays
28	**What did you have?**	past simple: *did, didn't* *have / had* questions: *what, where, who, when*	special occasions meals, snacks, presents, parties
29	**What did you do?**	past simple: *did, didn't* frequent irregular verbs: *went, saw, bought, got*	talking about the past, shopping, post, films
30	**Life events**	past simple: *did, didn't* regular verbs ending in *-ed* *was born, got married*	personal history narrative, biodata using the past tense

Extensions 1–30 152

Communication Activities 182

Transcripts 203

Grammar 212

Classroom language

Class work

Listen and repeat.

Open the book.

Close the book.

Pair work

Practise the conversation.

Ask and answer.

Make conversations.

Exercises

Tick.

1 Hello, my name's Anna.
2 Hello, my name's To
Underline.

1 Hello, my name's Anna.
2 Hello, my name's To
Circle.

Match.

1 Hello, my name's *Anna*
2 Hello, my name's ....
Complete the sentence.

1 Hello, (☐ I ☑ my) name's ...
2 Hello, (☐ I ☐ my) name's Tom
Choose the correct word.

Look at unit 4.

Look at page 13.

1 What's your name?

A Hello

1 Listen. ✱ 1.2

Listen and repeat.

2 Pair work.
▶ Hello, my name's (*Maria*).
◀ Hello, (*Maria*). My name's (*Tom*).
▶ Good to meet you, (*Tom*).
◀ Good to meet you, (*Maria*).

B Listening

1 **Listen. Match the conversations and the photos.
   Write the numbers on the photos.**

   ✱ 1.3
   ● Hi, what's your name?
   ■ Kate.

   ✱ 1.4
   ● What's her name?
   ■ I don't know.

   ✱ 1.5
   ● What's his name?
   ■ His name's Nick.

   ✱ 1.6
   ● Aah! What's her name?
   ■ His name's Ben.

2 **Ask three students.**
   ▶ Hi, what's your name?
   ◀ Hi, my name's (*Maria*).

3 **Complete the sentences with *his* or *her*.**
   .... name's David.
   .... name's Venus.

4 **Pair work. Ask and answer about students in your class.**
   ▶ What's her name?   ▶ What's his name?
   ◀ Her name's (*Maria*).   ◀ His name's (*Tom*).

C Numbers 0–9

1 Listen and repeat the numbers. (✱ 1.7)

0	1	2	3	4	5	6	7	8	9
zero/o	one	two	three	four	five	six	seven	eight	nine

2 Listen. (✱ 1.8)
- What's your phone number?
- o nine seven three seven, two four eight, five one six. What's your number?
- My number's o four nine six, eight o two, five five three.

3 Write the phone numbers.
His number's _ _ _ _ _ / _ _ _ / _ _ _
Her number's _ _ _ _ / _ _ _ / _ _ _

Ask and answer.
What's his phone number?
What's her phone number?

4 Listen and write the numbers.

(✱ 1.9) _____

(✱ 1.10) _____

(✱ 1.11) _____

(✱ 1.12) _____

D Language focus

What	's is	your his her my	name? number?

What's = What is

My His Her Your	name number	's is	Kate. Ben. 01865 346547. 0446 278990.

1 Complete the sentences.
My name .... David. What .... your phone number?
Hello, David. My number .... 792 5180.

2 Ask three students.

```
○  NAME .................................................
○  ✆ PHONE NUMBER ...............................

○  NAME .................................................
○  ✆ PHONE NUMBER ...............................

○  NAME .................................................
○  ✆ PHONE NUMBER ...............................
```

E Goodbye

1 Listen. ✱ 1.13
● Goodbye, Venus.
■ Goodbye, David.

2 Say goodbye to the students in your class.

See **Extension 1** p.152

2 Are you a student?

A Conversations

1 **Listen. Match the conversations and the photos.**
   * 1.14 ☐
   * 1.15 ☐
   * 1.16 ☐

   Practise the conversations.

* 1.14
- Excuse me ...
- Yes?
- Are you a student?
- No, I'm not. I'm a teacher.

* 1.15
- Is he a doctor?
- No, he isn't. He's a nurse.

UNIT TWO

(✷ 1.16)

- Excuse me! Are you Meg Taylor?
- Yes, I am.
- Hello, Ms Taylor. I'm Josh Stewart.
- Are you a journalist, Mr Stewart?
- Um, yes, I am …
- No questions. Goodbye!

2 Ask about photos 1 – 3. Change the words in *italics*.

Picture 1
- ▶ Is she a *teacher*?
- ◀ Yes, she is.
- ▶ Is he a *doctor*?
- ◀ No, he isn't. / I don't know.

student   teacher   doctor
nurse   journalist

B What's your job?

1 Write the numbers of the pictures.

Picture	☐	☐	☐	☐
Job	cleaner	scientist	shop assistant	doctor
Title	Mr	Miss / Ms	Mrs / Ms	Dr
Name	Wilson	Clark	Carter	Green

Look at the table. Listen and repeat. ✻ 1.17

2 Ask about the pictures.

Picture 4
- ▶ What's her name?
- ◀ Her name's Miss Clark.
- ▶ What's her job?
- ◀ She's a scientist.

3 Look in a dictionary. What's your job in English?

4 Make conversations.
- ▶ Hello. I'm (*Josh Stewart*). What's your name?
- ◀ Hello, (*Mr Stewart*). I'm (*Anna Clark*).
- ▶ Good to meet you, (*Miss Clark*). What's your job?
- ◀ I'm a (*scientist*). What's your job?
- ▶ I'm a (*journalist*).

C Language focus

Positive and negative

I	'm	a doctor.
	am	a teacher.
	'm not	a student.
You	're	
	are	
	aren't	
She	's	
He	is	
	isn't	

Questions

Are	you	a doctor?
		a teacher?
		a student?
Is	she	
	he	

What's	your	job?
	his	name?
	her	number?
	my	

Short answers

Yes, I am. / No, I'm not. NOT ~~Yes, I'm.~~
Yes, she is. / No, she isn't.
Yes, he is. / No, he isn't. NOT ~~Yes, he's.~~

Complete the sentences.

1 .... Mr Johnson a doctor?   No, he .... He .... a nurse.
2 .... you a teacher?   Yes, I ....
3 Is she .... journalist?   Yes, she ....
4 What .... her job?   ....'s a scientist.
5 Are .... a cleaner?   No, I'm ....

D Alphabet

1 Listen and repeat. ✱ 1.18

/iː/	B C D E G P T V
/e/	F L M N S X Z
/eɪ/	A H J K
/uː/	Q U W
/aɪ/	I Y
/əʊ/	O
/ɑː/	R

2 Listen. ✱ 1.19
- What's your name?
- I'm Dylan Jones.
- Can you spell that, please?
- Yes. Dylan, D-Y-L-A-N. Jones, J-O-N-E-S.

3 Practise spelling.
▶ What's your name?
◀ ……………………………………………………………… .

▶ Can you spell that?
◀ Yes. ……………………………………………………… .

4 Ask about students in your class.
▶ What's (*his / her*) name?
◀ ……………………………………………………………… .

▶ Can you spell that?
◀ Yes. ……………………………………………………… .

5 Classroom English. Listen and repeat. ✱ 1.20
/kən/ Can you spell that, please?
/kən/ Can you repeat that, please?
/kən/ Can you translate that, please?

E Listening

1. **Listen to 'Can you spell?'** ✱ 1.21

2. **Underline the right words.**
   1. His name's (Mr / Dr) Watson.
   2. He's a (medical doctor / scientist).
   3. Her name's (Mrs / Miss) Smith.
   4. She's a (cleaner / nurse).
   5. The right spelling is (journalist / journelist).
   6. Her answer is (right / wrong).

   Listen again and check.

COMMUNICATION

Student A Look at Activity 1 on p.182.
Student B Look at Activity 11 on p.192.

See **Extension 2** p.153

3 Where are you from?

A Personal information

1 **Look at the computer. Match the questions and the answers.**

   Question
   1 What's her first name?
   2 What's her family name?
   3 Is she married?
   4 What's her job?
   5 Where's she from?

   Answer
   A No, she isn't. She's single.
   B Lucia.
   C Rodrigues.
   D She's from Brazil.
   E She's a student.

   Listen and check. ✱ 1.22

2 **Listen. You can hear two sounds for *from*: stressed /frɒm/ and unstressed /frəm/. Underline the stressed examples.** ✱ 1.23
   1 Where's Lucia from?
   2 She's from Brazil.
   3 Where are you from?
   4 I'm from New York.

3 **Look at exercise 1. Write five questions with *you* or *your*. Ask your partner the five questions.**

B Country and nationality

Title _____
Name Lucia Rodrigues
Country Brazil
Nationality Brazilian

Title _____
Name Karl Brandt
Country Germany
Nationality German

Title _____
Name Maria Lopez
Country Spain
Nationality Spanish

Title _____
Name Paul Lefort
Country France
Nationality French

Title _____
Name Miki Tanaka
Country Japan
Nationality Japanese

1 **Look at the photos. Listen and write the titles.** (✻ 1.24)
   Listen again and repeat.

2 **Stress. Say the words. Then listen and check.** (✻ 1.25)

• ●	● • •	• ●	●	• ●
Brazil	Germany	Spain	France	Japan

• ● • •	● •	● •	●	• • ●
Brazilian	German	Spanish	French	Japanese

3 **Ask about the photos.**
   ▶ What nationality is Lucia?
   ◀ She's Brazilian.
   ▶ Where's she from?
   ◀ She's from Brazil.

C Welcome to the chat room

1 Listen and read. (✻ 1.26)

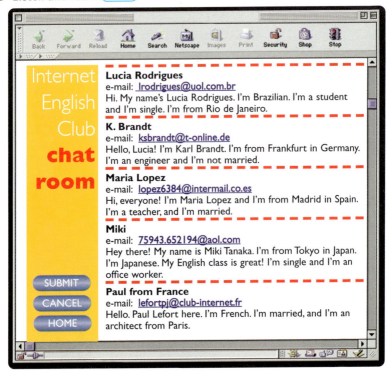

Lucia Rodrigues
e-mail: lrodrigues@uol.com.br
Hi. My name's Lucia Rodrigues. I'm Brazilian. I'm a student and I'm single. I'm from Rio de Janeiro.

K. Brandt
e-mail: ksbrandt@t-online.de
Hello, Lucia! I'm Karl Brandt. I'm from Frankfurt in Germany. I'm an engineer and I'm not married.

Maria Lopez
e-mail: lopez6384@intermail.co.es
Hi, everyone! I'm Maria Lopez and I'm from Madrid in Spain. I'm a teacher, and I'm married.

Miki
e-mail: 75943.652194@aol.com
Hey there! My name is Miki Tanaka. I'm from Tokyo in Japan. I'm Japanese. My English class is great! I'm single and I'm an office worker.

Paul from France
e-mail: lefortpj@club-internet.fr
Hello. Paul Lefort here. I'm French. I'm married, and I'm an architect from Paris.

2 Write the questions.

Question	Answer
	Karl Brandt.
	He's from Frankfurt.
	It's in Germany.
	He's an engineer.
	No, he isn't married. He's single.

Now ask about Maria.

3 Give short answers to these questions about Miki.
Is she French?
Is she from Tokyo?
Is Tokyo in Japan?
Is she a shop assistant?
Is she single?

Now ask about Paul. Give short answers.

D Language focus

Where are you from? I'm from (*London*).
What nationality are you? I'm (*English*).

Where's (*London*)? It's in (*England*).
Is (*Tokyo*) in (*Japan*)? Yes, it is. / No, it isn't.

Are you married? Yes, I am. / No, I'm not.
Are you (*English*)? No, I'm not. / Yes, I am.

He	's	**a t**eacher.
She		**a s**tudent.
I	'm	**an o**ffice worker.
You	're	**an e**ngineer.
		an architect.

1 Complete the sentences with *a* or *an*.
  1 Lucia is .... student.
  2 Karl is .... engineer.
  3 Maria is .... teacher.
  4 Miki is .... office worker.
  5 Paul is .... architect.

2 Underline the correct words.
  1 She's from (Spanish / Spain).
  2 (Where / What) nationality is he?
  3 (Where / Where's) Frankfurt?
  4 Rio de Janeiro's (from / in) Brazil.

E Writing

Write a message about you.

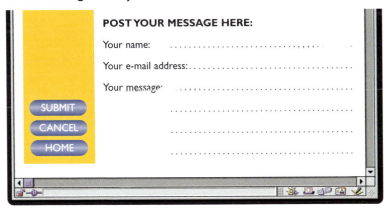

See **Extension 3** p.154

4 Hello, goodbye

A How are you?

1 **Listen. Complete the sentences.** (✱ 1.27)
   - Hello! How .... you?
   - I'm fine, thanks. And .... ?
   - Fine, ...

2 **Go around the class. Practise the conversation.**

3 **Practise again. Change these words.**
Hello → Hi
fine → very well
thanks → thank you

B Greetings

(* 1.28)
- Good morning, Jack.
- Good morning, Ms Robertson.

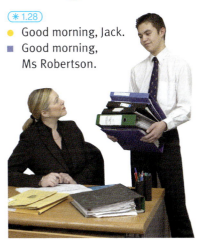

(* 1.29)
- Good afternoon.
- Good afternoon.
- Is Mr Green in?
- No, I'm sorry. He's out.

(* 1.30)
- Good evening, sir.
  Good evening, madam.
- Good evening.

(* 1.31)
- Goodnight, Tom.
- Goodnight.

1 **Listen. Then practise the conversations.**

2 **Translate these greetings into your language.**

   Hi   Hello   Good morning   Good afternoon   Good evening   Goodbye

3 **Put the words in the correct groups.**

   Good morning   Hi   Good afternoon   Good evening   Goodnight

'Hello' only	'Goodbye' only	'Hello' or 'Goodbye'

C I don't understand

1 Listen. (✱ 1.32)
- Excuse me ...
- Yes?
- Do you speak Spanish?
- Sorry. I don't speak Spanish. What's the problem?
- I'm sorry. Can you repeat that? I don't understand.

Now practise the conversation. Use these words.
French   German   Japanese   Italian

2 Listen. (✱ 1.33)

Yes.
Yes is an answer.

Yes?
Yes is a question.

3 Listen to these words in conversations.
Write a question mark (?) after the words with question intonation.

✱ 1.34	sorry	✱ 1.38	sorry
✱ 1.35	yes	✱ 1.39	excuse me
✱ 1.36	yes	✱ 1.40	Bill
✱ 1.37	excuse me	✱ 1.41	Maria

4 Punctuation. Add an apostrophe (') to these sentences.
1 Im fine, thanks.
2 I dont speak Italian.
3 Whats the problem?
4 Her names Anna.
5 Youre a student.

D Language focus

I	don't	know.	Do	you	speak	English?
		understand.				Spanish?
		speak (*English*).				French?

don't = do not

Make sentences.
understand. / Sorry, / don't / I
Sorry, I don't understand.
1 Japanese? / you / Do / speak
2 French. / don't / No, / speak / I
3 don't / sorry, / I / know. / I'm

E Song

1 **Listen and read.** ✱ 1.42

Hello, Goodbye
John Lennon and Paul McCartney

You say yes, I say no
You say stop, and I say go. go, go.
Oh, no! You say goodbye and I say hello
CHORUS
*Hello, hello, I don't know why you say goodbye
I say hello, hello, hello
I don't know why you say goodbye, I say hello*

I say high, you say low,
You say why?, and I say I don't know
Oh, no! You say goodbye and I say hello
(Hello, goodbye, hello, goodbye)
CHORUS

Why, why, why, why, why
Do you say goodbye?
Goodbye … bye … bye … bye …
Oh, no! You say goodbye and I say hello
CHORUS

You say yes (I say yes)
I say no (but I may mean no)
You say stop (I can stay …)
But I say go (… until it's time to go)
CHORUS

Hello, hello. I don't know why you
  say goodbye
I say hello … o … o … o … hello

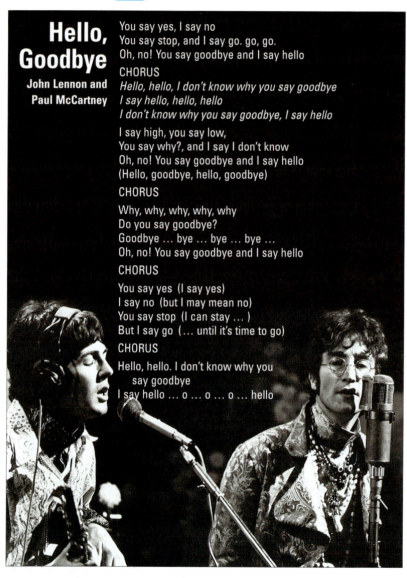

2 **Match the words and their opposites.**

1 yes   A go
2 hello   B low
3 high   C goodbye
4 stop   D no

3 **Find words in the song with the same sound.**

hell**o** /əʊ/

goodb**ye** /aɪ/

See **Extension 4** p.155

5 What is it?

A Numbers 10–20

1 Listen and repeat. (✱ 1.43)

10	11	12	13	14	15
ten	eleven	twelve	thirteen	fourteen	fifteen

16	17	18	19	20
sixteen	seventeen	eighteen	nineteen	twenty

2 Listening Bingo!
Write six numbers between 10 and 20 on the table. Listen and ~~cross out~~ the numbers. (✱ 1.44)

3 (Circle) the numbers in the song titles.

Twenty Flight Rock
Eddie Cochran

The Twelve Days of Christmas
Roger Whittaker

Only Sixteen
Ringo Starr

Twenty Miles
Chubby Checker

Eighteen Yellow Roses
Bobby Darin

Fourteen
Mad House

She's Nineteen Years Old
Muddy Waters

Ten Long Years
B.B. King

Eighteen with a Bullet
Pete Wingfield

Happy Birthday Sweet Sixteen
Neil Sedaka

Ten Green Bottles
Kirklees Junior Schools

Seventeen
The Sex Pistols

Fifteen Minutes
Kirsty MacColl

Thirteen Questions
Seatrain

The Eleven
The Grateful Dead

B What is it?

1 **Match the numbers and the words.**

- [ ] dictionary
- [ ] map
- [ ] passport
- [ ] identity card
- [ ] camera
- [ ] apple
- [ ] toothbrush
- [ ] phone
- [ ] ticket
- [ ] hat
- [ ] orange
- [ ] penknife
- [ ] watch
- [ ] pen
- [ ] film
- [ ] umbrella
- [ ] key
- [ ] backpack
- [ ] envelope
- [ ] towel

Now listen and check. (✱ 1.45)

2 **Listen again. Underline the words with *an*.**

C Language focus

a / an
a before the sound of a **consonant**
b c d f g h j k l m n p q r s t v w x y z

an before the sound of a **vowel**
a e i o u

Singular
What is it?
It	's	a	camera.
	is		watch.
	isn't	an	apple.
			orange.

Questions
| Is | it | a book? |
| | | an orange? |

Short answers
Yes, it is.
No, it isn't.

1 **Look at Language focus, *a / an*. Ask about the pictures.**
  ▶ What's number one?
  ◀ It's a backpack.
  ▶ What's number three?
  ◀ It's an apple.

2 **Game. Student B close your book. Student A say a number. Student B can you remember?**
  ▶ Number one.
  ◀ Is it a (*backpack*)?
  ▶ Yes, it is. / No, it isn't.

3 **Repeat the game. Student A close your book.**

UNIT FIVE

D What are they?

Plural		
What are they?		
They	're	cameras.
	are	watches.
	aren't	apples.
		oranges.

Questions			Short answers
Are	they	apples?	Yes, they are.
		oranges?	No, they aren't.

10 ☐

11 ☐

1 Listen. Match the conversations and the photos.
(✳ 1.46 - 1.50)

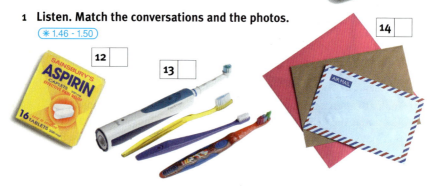

12 ☐   13 ☐   14 ☐

2 Listen. Then add the other words to the table. (✳ 1.51)

/s/	map**s**
/z/	camera**s**
/ɪz/	watch**es**

3 Pair work. Point at a picture. Ask and answer.
  ▶ What are they?
  ◀ They're (*keys*).

COMMUNICATION

Student A Look at Activity 2 on p.183.
Student B Look at Activity 12 on p.193.

E In your classroom

1 Point and ask your teacher about things in your classroom.
  ▶ What is it?   ▶ What are they?
  ◀ It's a / an ...   ◀ They're ...

2 Pair work. Ask about your classroom.

See **Extension 5** p.156

6 We're friends

A We're friends

1 Brad is Canadian. Look and listen. (✳ 1.52)

MY HOLIDAY IN IRELAND

Pat   Mary

Pat and Mary are Irish.
They're from Dublin.

We're friends. We're in a pub.

We're in a Chinese restaurant.
We're good friends!

2 Are these sentences true (✓) or false (✗) for you and your partner?
1 We're students.
2 We aren't British.
3 We're friends.
4 We're in a restaurant.
5 We're married.

3 Look at another pair of students.
Make sentences with *They're* or *They aren't* …

B Excuse me!

(✷ 1.53)

Amy Tea or coffee?
Matt Tea, please.
Amy Anything else?
Matt No, thanks.

(✷ 1.54)

Amy Excuse me ...
Waiter Just a minute, madam.
Amy We're in a hurry.
Two teas ...
Waiter Sorry, madam. We're busy.

(✷ 1.55)

Matt Excuse me! Waiter!
We're in a hurry!
Waiter Sorry, sir. We're busy!

(✷ 1.56)

Amy Matt, what's the phone number of the restaurant?
Matt I don't know, Amy.
Amy It's on the menu.
Matt Oh, yes. Here you are.

UNIT SIX 33

Tower Restaurant
19 London Road • Southampton
☎ (023) 8059 6248

MENU

✱ 1.57

Amy 023 8059 6248. Hello? Tower Restaurant? We're by the window. Two teas, please. We're in a hurry!

1 **Listen. Pair work. Practise the conversations.**

2 **Ask about the conversations. Give short answers.**
Is her name Amy?
Is his name Pat?
Are they in a restaurant?
Are they by the door?
Are they in a hurry?
Are the waiters busy?

C Language focus

Positive and negative

We	're	busy.
You	are	in a hurry.
They	aren't	British.
	are not	waiters.

Questions

Are	you	busy?
	they	in a hurry?
	we	British?
		waiters?

Short answers

Yes, you are.
No, we aren't.

Answer your teacher.

Teacher   Are you Spanish?
Class   Yes, we are. / No, we aren't.

Are you students?
Are you in a restaurant?
Are you in an office?
Are you in a classroom?
Are you busy?

D Where ... ?

Where are they?
in a restaurant, **in** a shop, **in** an office, **in** a bar
by the window, **by** the door

in a hurry / **on** the menu

1 **Complete the sentences.**
Amy and Matt are .... a restaurant. They're .... the window. They're .... a hurry. The phone number is .... the menu.

2 **Pair work. Make sentences about you and your partner with *We* ...**
Where are you?
Are you by the window or by the door?
What nationality are you?
Where are you from?

E Yes, please / No, thanks

1 **Complete the conversation with *please* or *thanks*.**
 - Tea?
 - No, ...
 - Coffee?
 - Yes, ...
 - Anything else?
 - No, ...

2 *Tea* and *coffee* are drinks. Do you know more drinks? e.g. *Cola*.

3 **Practise the conversation. Use words from exercise 2.**

See **Extension 6** p.157

7 Take out

A Next, please

1 Look at the menu. Are the words the same in your language?

2 Listen. Then practise the conversation. (✱ 1.58)

Server	Next, please.
Customer	Chicken nuggets, fries and a cola, please.
Server	Regular or large cola?
Customer	Regular, please.
Server	Eat in or take out?
Customer	Take out.
Server	Anything else?
Customer	No, thanks.
Server	There you go. Four fifty.
Customer	Thanks.
Server	You're welcome … Next!

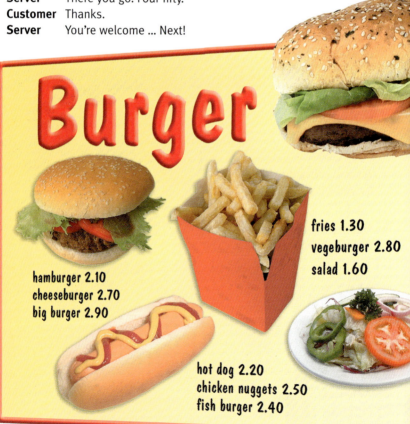

fries 1.30
vegeburger 2.80
salad 1.60

hamburger 2.10
cheeseburger 2.70
big burger 2.90

hot dog 2.20
chicken nuggets 2.50
fish burger 2.40

B Numbers 10–90

1 Listen and repeat. (✱ 1.59)

10	20	30	40	50	60	70	80	90
ten	twenty	thirty	forty	fifty	sixty	seventy	eighty	ninety

2 Look at the stress.

thirteen　　thirty

Listen. Circle the number you hear. (✱ 1.60)

thirteen
13 / 30

A 19 / 90
B 18 / 80
C 14 / 40

D 13 / 30
E 15 / 50
F 16 / 60

G 17 / 70
H 15 / 50
I 16 / 60

J 14 / 40
K 17 / 70
L 18 / 80

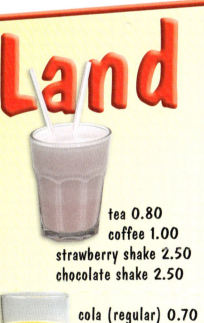

tea 0.80
coffee 1.00
strawberry shake 2.50
chocolate shake 2.50
cola (regular) 0.70
cola (large) 1.40
mineral water 1.60
orange juice 1.70

C Conversations

1 Pair work. Ask about the menu.
▶ Tea, please.
◀ Eighty (pence).
▶ Chicken nuggets, please.
◀ Two fifty.

**2 Listen to the examples.
Pair work.** (✱ 1.61)
▶ Fries, please.
◀ Here you are.
▶ How much is that?
◀ One thirty, please.

Pair work. (✱ 1.62)
▶ An orange juice, please.
◀ Here you are. Anything to eat?
▶ No, thanks.
◀ One seventy.

Pair work. (✱ 1.63)
▶ A burger, please.
◀ There you go. Anything to drink?
▶ No, thank you.
◀ Two ten, please.

UNIT SEVEN

D Listening

Prices

one	–	fifteen
	pound	sixteen
	euro	twenty
	dollar	thirty
two	–	fifty
five	pounds	sixty
ten	euros	eighty
	dollars	ninety

1 Listen. Write on the cash register.

✱ 1.64

Tick (✓) the food and drinks.
How much is that? ....

✱ 1.65

Cross (✗) the food and drinks.
How much is that? ....

✱ 1.66

Circle the food and drinks.
How much is that? ....

2 Role play a conversation. Use words from the menu on p.36.

E Excuse me ...

1 Listen. ✱ 1.67

Woman Excuse me, can I have the ketchup, please?
Man Here you are. And the salt?
Woman Yes, please.
Man And the pepper?
Woman No, thank you.

Practise the conversation.

2 Listen to the example. Pair work. ✱ 1.68

▶ Excuse me, can I have the sugar?
◀ Here you are. And the milk?
▶ Yes, please.

F Language focus

Expressions
Regular **or** large? Eat in **or** take out?
Here you are. / There you go.
Anything (else? / to eat? / to drink?)
Can I have (*the milk*), please?
How much is that? → One fifty.
Thank you. / Thanks. → You're welcome.

Match the questions and the answers.

Question	Answer
1 Eat in or take out?	A Fries, please.
2 Anything to drink?	B Here you are.
3 Anything to eat?	C Four eighty.
4 Regular or large cola?	D Take out, please.
5 Can I have the pepper?	E Large, please.
6 How much is that?	F Cola, please.

See **Extension 7** p.158

8 What colour is it?

21 a colour printer

22 yellow lines

23 a black and white film

25 a green light

24 blue jeans

26 a red card

A Colours

1 **Listen. Ask about the pictures.** ✱ 1.69
   ▶ Twenty-one. What is it?
   ◀ It's a colour printer.
   ▶ Twenty-two. What are they?
   ◀ They're yellow lines.

2 **Ask about the pictures.**
   21 Is it a colour printer or a black and white printer?
   22 What colour are the lines?
   23 Is it a colour film or a black and white film?
   24 What colour are the jeans?
   25 What colour is the light?
   26 Is it a red card or a yellow card?

3 **Listen. Repeat the colours.** ✱ 1.70

black   grey   white   blue   green   yellow   brown   red   pink

B Hot and cold

1 Complete the spaces with these words.

| new | cold | big | old | small | hot |

27 a .... tap
28 a .... car
29 .... shoes
30 a .... tap
31 a .... car
32 .... shoes

Now listen and check. ✱ 1.71

2 Ask about the pictures.
▶ Twenty-seven. What is it?
◀ It's a tap.
▶ Is it hot or cold?
◀ It's hot.

▶ Twenty-nine. What are they?
◀ They're shoes.
▶ Are they new or old?
◀ They're new.

3 Ask about the colours.
▶ What colour is the hot tap?
◀ It's red.
▶ What colour are the new shoes?
◀ They're black.

C Language focus

Adjectives
- Adjectives are the same for singular and plural.
  a new shoe, new shoes, red cars NOT *reds cars*.
  It's new. They're new.
- Adjectives are the same for *he, she, it, they*.
  It's cold. He's cold. She's cold. They're cold.
- Adjectives come after the verb *to be*.
  It's big. They're green. She's Spanish.
- Adjectives come before nouns.
  a pink car, blue jeans NOT *a car pink, jeans blue*.

1 Listen. This is from a football match.

   Complete the spaces with colours. ✱1.72

   Now check with your partner.

2 Circle the adjectives. Check in the Transcript on page 205.

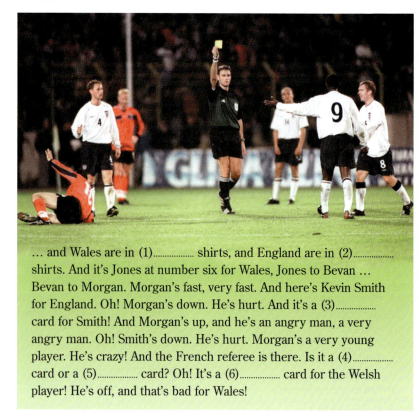

… and Wales are in (1)................ shirts, and England are in (2)................ shirts. And it's Jones at number six for Wales, Jones to Bevan … Bevan to Morgan. Morgan's fast, very fast. And here's Kevin Smith for England. Oh! Morgan's down. He's hurt. And it's a (3)................ card for Smith! And Morgan's up, and he's an angry man, a very angry man. Oh! Smith's down. He's hurt. Morgan's a very young player. He's crazy! And the French referee is there. Is it a (4)................ card or a (5)................ card? Oh! It's a (6)................ card for the Welsh player! He's off, and that's bad for Wales!

D Talk about colours

a red heart = love

1 Match the words from box A and box B.

A		B
a red tap		no parking
a blue tap		stop
a green light	is for	cold water
a red light		go
a yellow line		hot water

2 Look at the examples. Are they the same in your language?

red
- an angry person
- a hot thing

green
- a green salad
- the environment – the Green Party in politics

blue
- an unhappy person
- cold things
- the light on a British police car is blue

yellow
- a Smiley is yellow

3 Think of ideas for the colours.
- ▶ green
- ◀ a green salad

4 Talk about colours.
What colour is (*your toothbrush*)?
What colour are (*her shoes*)?

See **Extension 8** p.159

9 This is your room ...

A Room 1330

1 **Listen.** (✱ 1.73) (✱ 1.74) (✱ 1.75)
   Pearl is a famous American rock singer. She's in a hotel in London.

2 <u>Underline</u> **these words in the conversations.**
   great   good   very nice   OK   fine   right

3 **Practise the conversations.**

(✱ 1.73)

Porter This is room 1330. It's a beautiful suite.
Pearl Yeah. Very nice.
Porter There's a living room, there's a bedroom, and there's a bathroom.
Pearl Great. Thanks.
Porter And there's a widescreen TV, and a DVD player.
Pearl Oh, right. Yeah. Good. Thank you.

(✱ 1.74)

Porter There's a bath and a shower.
Pearl Fine.
Porter And there are some towels.
Pearl Hmm. Are there any large towels?
Porter Yes, there are some large towels here.
Pearl Oh. There aren't any bathrobes.
Porter No, there aren't. I'm very sorry.
Pearl Hmm.

(✱ 1.75)

Porter There's a mini-bar. Here's the key. And …
Pearl Yes, yes. I'm sorry, I'm very tired.
Porter And the air-conditioning controls are by the door … and …
Pearl OK! OK! Look, this is for you … goodnight.
Porter Oh, thank you, madam. Um … can I have your autograph, please?

B Language focus

There is ... / There are ...

There	's	a	bed.	There	isn't	a	bed.
	is	an	armchair.			an	armchair.
	are	some	armchairs.		aren't	any	beds.
		two	beds.				armchairs.

Questions

Is	there	a	bed?
		an	armchair?
Are		any	beds?
			armchairs?

Short answers
Yes, there is.
No, there isn't.
Yes, there are.
No, there aren't.

Room 1330 = Room thirteen thirty

1 Complete the sentences with *is* or *are*.
Room 1330 is a suite. There (1)................. three rooms. There's a living room, a bedroom, and a bathroom. In the living room there (2)................. a mini-bar. There's a TV and a DVD player. There (3)................. a bath and a shower in the bathroom. There (4)................. two beds in the bedroom.

2 Complete the sentences with *some* or *any*.
1 There are .... towels in the bathroom.
2 Are there .... bathrobes?
3 No, there aren't .... bathrobes.

3 Listen. Write the room numbers. (✻ 1.76)
A ....   B ....   C ....   D ....
E ....   F ....   G ....   H ....

C A hotel room

1 Read the text. Put the words in bold in the boxes. (✻ 1.77)

2 Answer these questions with short answers.
1 Is there an armchair?
2 Is there a DVD player?
3 Are there any lights on the wall?
4 Are there any towels in the room?

3 Tick (✓) the correct words.
1 'Where are the lights?'   '(☐ They're ☐ There are) on the wall.'
2 'Are there any towels?'   'No, (☐ they ☐ there) aren't.'
3 'Are there any chairs?'   'Yes, (☐ there ☐ they) are.'
4 'Are the beds double or single?'   '(☐ They're ☐ There are) double beds.'

Now listen and check. (✻ 1.78)

UNIT NINE

There are two double **beds** in the room. There are two small **lights** on the **wall**. There's a white **telephone** and a **radio**. There's a **table** and there are two **chairs**. There's an **armchair**. There's a **wardrobe**. There's a colour **television**. There's a **picture** on the wall. There's a blue **carpet** on the floor.

COMMUNICATION

Student A Look at Activity 3 on p.184.
Student B Look at Activity 13 on p.194.

D Writing

Describe a room in your home.

See **Extension 9** p.160

10 Shopping

A Shopping for clothes

1 **Ask and answer.**
   ▶ How much is the sweatshirt?
   ◀ It's thirty-six ninety-nine.

T-shirt £17.50
- purple
- black
- white

sweatshirt £36.99
- dark blue
- red
- dark green

UNIT TEN

2 Listen. (* 1.79)

Assistant Can I help you?
Customer Yes, I'm looking for a *sweatshirt*.
Assistant What colour?
Customer *Dark blue.*
Assistant What size?
Customer *Medium.*
Assistant Here you are.
Customer Thanks. How much is it?
Assistant *Thirty-six ninety-nine.*

3 Make conversations. Change the words in *italics*.

Sizes
S = small   L = large
M = medium   XL = extra large

top £28.25
- orange
- pink
- yellow

shirt £57.95
- light blue
- grey
- light green

B Shopping for shoes

1 Repeat the numbers. (✱ 1.80)

Large numbers
100 – one hundred
540 – five hundred and forty
2000 – two thousand
3800 – three thousand eight hundred
4691 – four thousand six hundred and ninety-one

boots £155.15	trainers £119.99	shoes £125.98
light brown	white	black
black	black	brown
dark brown	dark blue	

Sizes (European)
Women	36 37 38 39 40 41
Men	40 41 42 43 44 45 46 47

2 Ask about the pictures.

▶ How much are the shoes?
◀ They're one hundred and fifty-five fifteen.

3 Listen. (✱ 1.81)

Assistant Can I help you?
Customer Yes, I'm looking for some boots.
Assistant What colour?
Customer *Light brown.*
Assistant What size?
Customer *Forty-one.*
Assistant Here you are.
Customer Thanks. How much are they?
Assistant *One hundred and fifty-five fifteen.*

Now make conversations. Change the words in *italics*.

C Listening

1 **Match the conversations and the pictures.**
   ✱ 1.82 ☐   ✱ 1.83 ☐   ✱ 1.84 ☐   ✱ 1.85 ☐

2 **Listen again. Write the size and colour. Write (?) for 'don't know'.**

	Item	Size	Colour
✱ 1.82			
✱ 1.83			
✱ 1.84			
✱ 1.85			

3 **Pair work. Ask about the pictures. Point and make sentences.**
   ▶ Who is (*the sweatshirt*) for?
   ◀ It's for (*her*).
   ▶ Who are (*the shoes*) for?
   ◀ They're for (*him*).

D Language focus

How much	is	it?
What size		the top?
What colour	are	they?
		the shoes?

I'm / You're / He's / She's a student.
The book is for **me** / **you** / **him** / **her**.
My / **Your** / **His** / **Her** name's Smith.

Subject pronouns	I	you	he	she
Object pronouns	me	you	him	her
Possessive adjectives	my	your	his	her

Questions
Who	is	it	for?
	's		
	are	they	

Short answers
It's	for	me.
		you.
They're		her.
		him.

1 **Underline the object pronouns in these sentences.**
   1 No, the milk isn't for me. It's for her.
   2 The tea isn't for you. It's for him.
   3 Is it his sweatshirt, or is it her sweatshirt?
   4 She's nice. Her friends aren't!
   5 Sorry, is it your coffee?
   6 No, my coffee is on the table.
   7 Good morning. An orange juice for me, and a milkshake for him.

2 (Circle) **the possessive adjectives in the sentences.**

3 **Match the questions and answers.**

   Questions
   1 What size is the top, please?
   2 Can I help you?
   3 Where are my grey trousers?
   4 Who are the trainers for?
   5 How much are they?
   6 What colour is her top?

   Answers
   A Yes, I'm looking for a top.
   B They're for her.
   C Twenty-five ninety-nine.
   D Medium.
   E Light blue.
   F They're in the wardrobe.

E How much? / What colour?

1 **Ask and answer.**
   - How much is the pink skirt?
   - It's (*thirty-seven sixty*).
   - How much are the yellow trousers?
   - They're (*eighty-four ninety-five*).

2 **Ask about clothes in your classroom. Point and ask.**
   - What colour's (*her dress*)?
   - It's (*light green*).
   - What colour are (*his jeans*)?
   - They're (*dark blue*).

COMMUNICATION
Student A Look at Activity 4 on p.185.
Student B Look at Activity 14 on p.195.

See **Extension 10** p.161

11 What have you got?

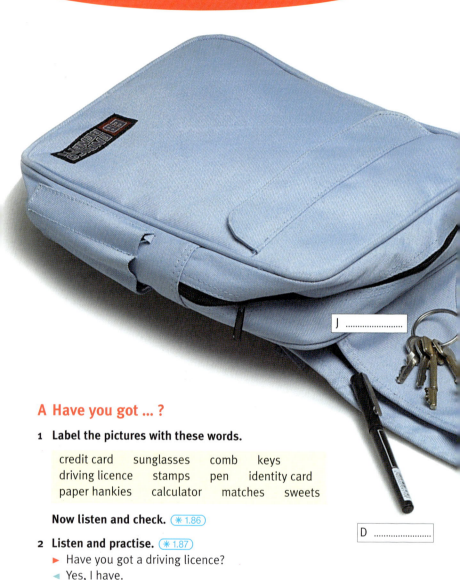

A Have you got ... ?

1 Label the pictures with these words.

credit card	sunglasses	comb	keys
driving licence	stamps	pen	identity card
paper hankies	calculator	matches	sweets

Now listen and check. (✱ 1.86)

2 Listen and practise. (✱ 1.87)
- ▶ Have you got a driving licence?
- ◀ Yes, I have.
- ▶ Have you got any keys?
- ◀ No, I haven't.

3 What have you got in your bag, or in your pocket? Ask about the things in the pictures. Put (✓) for yes, (✗) for no. Have you got anything else?

UNIT ELEVEN

K ....
C ....
A *credit card*
L ....
G ....
I ....
B ....
E ....
H ....
F ....

B Has she got ... ?

1 **Listen and practise.** (*1.88)
   ▶ Has she got a credit card?
   ◀ Yes, she has.
   ▶ Has he got any matches?
   ◀ No, he hasn't.

2 **Change partners. Ask about your partner's first partner.**

3 **Talk about your class.**
   (*Maria*)'s got (*an identity card*).
   (*David*) hasn't got (*an identity card*).
   (*David*)'s got some (*keys*).
   (*Maria*) hasn't got any (*keys*).

C Language focus

Positive

I	've	got	**a** credit card.
You	have		**an** ID card.
We			**some** keys.
They			
He	's		
She	has		

Negative

I	haven't	got	**a** credit card.
You	have not		**an** ID card.
We			**any** keys.
They			
He	hasn't		
She	has not		

Questions

Have	you	got	**a** credit card?
	we		**an** ID card?
	they		**any** keys?
	I		
Has	he		
	she		

Short answers

Yes, (I) have. / No, (we) haven't.
Yes, (he) has. / No, (he) hasn't.

1 Listen to the pronunciation of *have* and *has* in these sentences. Then listen and repeat. (✱ 1.89)

The sounds are unstressed in these sentences.
1 /həv/ Have you got a pen?
2 /həz/ Has he got any stamps?
3 /həv/ Have they got a car?
4 /həz/ Has she got a phone?

The sounds are stressed in these sentences.
5 /hæz/ Yes, he has.
6 /hæv/ Yes, I have.
7 /hæz/ Yes, she has.
8 /hæv/ Yes, we have.

2 Make sentences with
+ 've got / 's got
− haven't got / hasn't got
? Have (*you*) got ... ? / Has (*she*) got ... ?

1 (+) I / some new trainers
2 (+) she / a pink top
3 (−) we / a big car
4 (−) he / any boots
5 (?) they / any tickets
6 (?) the shop / any stamps

UNIT ELEVEN 57

D What have they got?

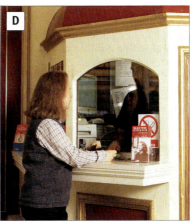

1 Listen. Match the conversations and the photos.

✳ 1.90 ☐   ✳ 1.91 ☐   ✳ 1.92 ☐   ✳ 1.93 ☐

2 **Match the words and the pictures.**

landing card ☐   three coins ☐
credit card ☐   driving licence ☐

E Reading

1 Read the texts.

(✻ 1.94)

> He's on a plane to England. He hasn't got an EU passport. He's got a Japanese passport. He hasn't got a pen.

(✻ 1.95)

> He's at a ticket office. He's got a credit card. It's American Express.

(✻ 1.96)

> She's at a nightclub. She's over 21. She hasn't got an ID card, but it's OK. She's got her driving licence. There's a photo of her on the licence.

(✻ 1.97)

> He hasn't got three coins for the photo machine. She's got three coins. He hasn't got a comb.

2 Look at the contraction 's in the texts.

Sometimes 's means *is*. Underline the examples of *is*.

Sometimes 's means *has*. Circle the examples of *has*.

F Survey

1 Ask three students. Put (✓) for yes, (✗) for no.

2 Add two more questions.

ARE YOU A TECHNOPHILE?

Have you got …?	1	2	3
a computer	☐	☐	☐
an Internet link	☐	☐	☐
a mobile phone	☐	☐	☐
a DVD player	☐	☐	☐
an MP3 player	☐	☐	☐
a games console (e.g. PlayStation)	☐	☐	☐
a digital camera	☐	☐	☐

See **Extension 11** p.162

12 Families

A Names

1 Ask and answer.
Have you got any brothers or sisters?
How old are they?
What are their names?
What are popular names in your country?

2 Look at the most popular names for babies in Britain in 2000. Listen and repeat. ✱ 2.02

Boys
1 Jack /dʒæk/
2 Thomas /ˈtɒməs/
3 James /dʒeɪmz/
4 Joshua /ˈdʒɒʃuːə/
5 Daniel /ˈdænjəl/

Girls
1 Chloe /ˈkləʊi/
2 Emily /ˈeməli/
3 Megan /ˈmegən/
4 Charlotte /ˈʃɑːlət/
5 Jessica /ˈdʒesɪkə/

B Our family

1 Listen and read.

Charlotte ✳ 2.03
My name's Charlotte. I'm married and my husband's name is James. We've got two children. Our daughter Jessica is four. She's got a baby brother, Joshua. He's nine months old. My brother's name is Tom and his wife is Megan. They've got two children. My nephew's name is Daniel, and my niece's name is Chloe. My father's name is Jack. My mother's name is Emily.

Daniel ✳ 2.04
I've got a sister. Her name's Chloe. And I've got two cousins. Their names are Jessica and Joshua. Jessica is four. Joshua's a baby. He's very noisy. My grandad's name is Jack, and my grandma's name is Emily. My aunt's name is Charlotte. She's married to my Uncle James.

Emily ✳ 2.05
I'm a grandmother. Jack and I have got two children and four grandchildren, two granddaughters and two grandsons. Megan is Tom's wife, and James is Charlotte's husband. Joshua is the baby. He's Jessica's brother.

2 Write the names on the family tree.

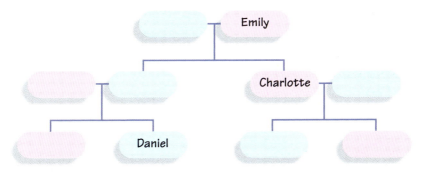

3 Put the words in the correct groups.

mother   son   daughter   child   grandparents   sister   brother   nephew   cousin   aunt   father   niece   single parent   uncle   grandfather   grandmother   grandson   granddaughter   children   parents   wife   husband

Female	mother
Male	
Male or female	

4 Complete sentence A. Then write sentence B.

A Chloe is Daniel**'s** sister.
B She's **his** sister.

1 **A** .... is Megan's husband.
  B ....
2 **A** .... is Tom's daughter.
  B ....
3 **A** .... is Megan and Tom's son.
  B ....
4 **A** .... is Joshua's aunt.
  B ....

5 Ask and answer.

Who is Jessica's uncle?
Who is her grandfather?
Who is Daniel's aunt?
Who is his grandmother?

Ask more questions about the family.

6 Make questions with *How many?*

How many children has Emily got?
How many grandchildren has Emily got?

C Language focus

Possessive ('s)

He's Megan**'s** husband.
She's James**'s** wife.
My nephew**'s** name is Peter.

Plural
My *nieces*' names are Jessica and Anna.

Irregular plural
The *children's* names are Daniel and Chloe.

Possessive adjectives

Plural
Our cousins' names are Anna and Paul.
Their names are Anna and Paul.
Hello, sir, madam. Where are **your** passports?

Question words

Who is Tom's sister?
How many brothers has she got?
How many children have they got?
How old are they?

Tick (✓) the correct words.
1 Are (☐ their ☐ they're) names Jack and Chloe?
2 (☐ We're ☐ Our) from England.
3 (☐ Your ☐ You're) passports are here.
4 She's (☐ John's ☐ John) sister.
5 (☐ We're ☐ Our) son's name is Dan.
6 They're Tom (☐ 's ☐ is) children.

D Your family

1. **Listen. Then repeat.** ✱ 2.06
   - Are you married?
   - Yes, I am. My husband's name is Thomas.
   - Have you got any brothers or sisters?
   - No, I haven't got any brothers or sisters. I'm an only child.

   - Have you got any brothers or sisters?
   - Yes, I've got a brother and two sisters.

   - How many sisters have you got?
   - I've got two sisters.
   - What are your parents' names?
   - Their names are David and Anna.

2. **Draw your family tree. Tell your partner about your family.**

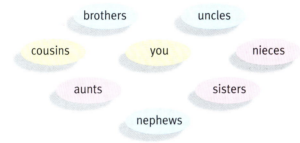

brothers · uncles · cousins · you · nieces · aunts · sisters · nephews

3. **Change partners. Ask about your first partner's family.**
   Has she got any sisters?
   How many sisters has she got?
   What (is her sister's name / are her sisters' names)?

E Writing

Write about your family.

See **Extension 12** p.163

13 Instructions

A Benny's day

Look at the cartoon. Match the sentences and the pictures. Write A to H on the pictures.

A Say 'please'.
B Turn off the TV, Benny.
C Don't forget your lunch.
D Be careful, Benny!
E Sit down, kids.
F Eat your breakfast, Benny.
G Give me the comic. Turn off the light.
H Say 'thank you'.

Now listen and check.

B Language focus

Verbs
look, *listen*, *be* are verbs.

	Imperative	Negative imperative
to look	Look	Don't look.
to listen	Listen	Don't listen.
to be	Be (*careful*)!	Don't be (*angry*).

Imperatives are for instructions. *Sit down!*
Say 'please' for requests. *Sit down, please. / Please sit down.*

Subject pronoun	Possessive adjective	Object pronoun
I	my	me
you	your	you
he	his	him
she	her	her
we	our	us
they	their	them

Complete the sentences with these words.

me   them   us   him   her

C Instructions

1 Tick (✓) the instructions you understand. Add more instructions.

- ☐ Open your books.
- ☐ Close your books.
- ☐ Listen and repeat.
- ☐ Don't write.
- ☐ Work in pairs.
- ☐ Read the conversation.
- ☐ Say that in English.
- ☐ Look at the picture.

2 Are these instructions true for your English class?

Turn off your mobile phone.
Don't speak your language in class.
Say 'please' and 'thank you'.
Don't translate.
Don't eat or drink in class.
Speak English in class.
Don't write in your book.
Don't look at your partner's homework.
Write new words in your notebook.

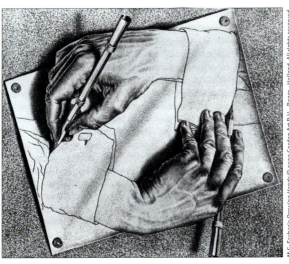

M.C. Escher's *Drawing Hands* © 2002 Cordon Art B.V. - Baarn - Holland. All rights reserved.

3 Listen, write, and draw. ✱ 2.08

4 Groups of three. Listen and do.
- ✱ 2.09 Student A
- ✱ 2.10 Student B
- ✱ 2.11 Student C

5 Write eight instructions for your partner. Use words from the box. Add more instructions.
Give your partner the instructions.

Stand up.	Sit down.	Open (*the door*).
Close (*the window*).	Turn on the light.	Turn off the light.
Go out.	Come in.	Look at (*her*).
Say (*hello*).	Go to (*the board*).	Draw (*a picture*).
Write (*your name*).	Give me (*your pen*).	

D Song

This is an old American blues song. Listen and read. (* 2.12)

Close your book. Listen again.

'Baby Please Don't Go'
Big Joe Williams

Oh, baby please don't go
Oh, baby please don't go
Oh, baby please don't go
back to New Orleans
because I love you so

Turn your lamp* down low
Turn your lamp down low
Turn your lamp down low
because I love you so
Baby please don't go

They've got me way down here
They've got me way down here
They've got me way down here
by the rolling fog*
treat me like a dog
Baby please don't go

* lamp = light
* by the rolling fog = in the Mississippi Delta, where there's fog. He's in prison.

See **Extension 13** p.164

14 Where do you live?

A I live ...

1. **Listen to Jade. Tick (✓) the true sentences.** ✻ 2.13

   ☐ I live in London.
   ☐ I don't live in London.
   ☐ I work in London.
   ☐ I don't work in London.
   ☐ I work in a hospital.
   ☐ I don't work in a hospital.

2. **Jade is at a party in London. Listen and underline the questions you hear.** ✻ 2.14

   Do you live in London?
   Do you live in Southend?
   Do you work in Southend?
   Do you work in London?
   Do you work in a hospital?
   Do you work in a hotel?

3. **Look at the underlined questions above. What are Jade's answers?**
   Write 'Y' for *Yes, I do*.
   Write 'N' for *No, I don't*.

B She lives ...

1 Complete the sentences.

Jade Butler lives in (1)................. . She lives in a flat. She doesn't work in (2)................. . She works in (3)................. . She's a receptionist and she works in a (4)................. .

Now listen and check. (✱ 2.15)

2 Choose the correct answers.

Does she live in London?
☐ Yes, she does.   ☐ No, she doesn't.

Does she work in London?
☐ Yes, she does.   ☐ No, she doesn't.

Now listen and check. (✱ 2.16)

3 Ask and answer about Jade. Change the words in *italics*.
▶ Does she live in *Southend*?
◀ Yes, she does.

Southend   *a flat*   *a hotel*   *a hospital*

C Language focus

The present simple

Positive

I	work	in	London.
You	live		a big city.
We			
They			
He	works		
She	lives		

Negative

I	don't	work	in	London.
You	do not	live		a big city.
We				
They				
He	doesn't			
She	does not			

Questions

Do	you	work	in	London?
	we	live		a big city?
	they			
	I			
Does	she			
	he			

Short answers

Yes,	I	do.
No,	you	don't.
	we	
	they	
	she	does.
	he	doesn't.

Where do you (*work*)?   Where does she (*live*)?

1 Listen.

(✱ 2.17)

Mike lives in New York City. He goes to Columbia University. His parents don't live in New York. They live in Boston.

(✱ 2.18)

Amy lives in Australia. She lives with her mother. Her mother works in Sydney. Amy doesn't work. She goes to school.

2 Answer the questions.

Where does Mike live?
Does he go to Harvard University?

Do his parents live in New York?
Where do they live?

Ask and answer about Amy.

3 Complete the sentences with *go* or *goes*.

1 He .... to Oxford University.
2 He doesn't .... to French classes.
3 We .... to English classes.
4 They don't .... to university.
5 She .... to college.
6 Does she .... to Spanish classes?
7 Do you .... to school?

D Choose a text

1 Complete the sentences. Then tick (✓) the boxes. Don't show your partner!

Their names are .... (male name) and .... (female name).

They've got ...

- ☐ a son
- ☐ a daughter 
- ☐ six children 
- ☐ a dog 

They live in ...

- ☐ a big house
- ☐ a small house 
- ☐ a flat 
- ☐ a mobile home 

He / She works ...

- ☐ in an office
- ☐ for Rolls-Royce 
- ☐ at home 
- ☐ at McDonald's 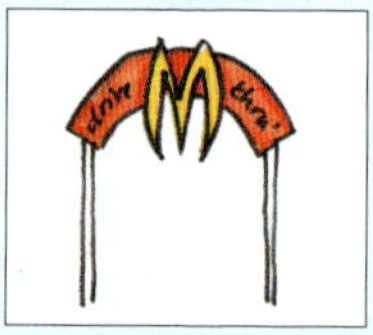

He / She ...

- ☐ hasn't got a job
- ☐ goes to college 
- ☐ is a student 
- ☐ is an astronaut 

2 Pair work. A ask B about his / her text. Then answer B's questions.
What are their names?
How many children have they got?
Do they live in a big house?
Does she work in an office?
Does he go to college?

E Survey

1 Pair work. Ask the questions. Tick (✓) the answers.

A Do you ... ?
- ☐ work
- ☐ go to college
- ☐ go to school
- ☐ go to university
- ☐ I haven't got a job.

B Do you live ... ?
- ☐ with your parents
- ☐ with your family
- ☐ with friends
- ☐ with your partner
- ☐ alone

C Do you work ... ?
- ☐ in an office
- ☐ in a factory
- ☐ in a hotel
- ☐ in a hospital
- ☐ in a school
- ☐ in a bank
- ☐ at home
- ☐ in a restaurant
- ☐ for (name of company)

D Where do you live?
- ☐ in a flat
- ☐ in a house

E Do you live in a ... ?
- ☐ big city
- ☐ town
- ☐ suburb
- ☐ village

F Do you work in your home town?
- ☐ Yes
- ☐ No

2 Pair work. Change partners. Ask questions about your first partner.
- ▶ Does (he / she) work?
- ◀ No, he doesn't. He goes to college.

3 Ask about your partner's family and friends.
Where does your (mother / father) work?
Where does your sister live?

F Writing

Write true sentences about you.

See **Extension 14** p.165

15 Times

A What time is it?

1 **Match the times to the clocks.**
   - ☐ twelve fifty-five
   - ☐ one fifteen
   - ☐ two forty-five
   - ☐ three ten
   - ☐ four twenty-five
   - ☐ five fifty
   - ☐ six forty
   - ☐ seven o five *
   - ☐ eight o'clock
   - ☐ nine twenty
   - ☐ ten thirty-five
   - ☐ eleven thirty

   * Write 7.05.
   Say 'seven "o" five'.

A

2 **Listen and repeat the times.** (✱ 2.19)

3 **Ask and answer about the clocks.** (✱ 2.20)
   ▶ What time is it?
   ◀ It's one fifteen.

4 **Ask three students.**
   What time is it now?

F

G

I

H

UNIT FIFTEEN

B Opening hours

1 **Look at the Tesco sign. Listen and repeat the days of the week.** (✱ 2.21)

2 **Listen. Match the conversations and the places A to I.**

Conversation	2.22	2.23	2.24	2.25	2.26	2.27	2.28	2.29	2.30
Place	☐	☐	☐	☐	☐	☐	☐	☐	☐

3 **Find this information.**
   1 What time does the bank open?
   2 What time does the post office close?
   3 How many hours does the superstore open on weekdays?
   4 Does the government office open at ten o'clock?
   5 Does the pub open at 11.00 a.m. on Sundays?
   6 What time does the tourist information centre open?
   7 Is the library open or closed on Wednesdays?
   8 How many abbreviations for 'Thursday' are there?

A superstore

B office

C post office

UNIT FIFTEEN

D bank

E pub

G tourist information centre

H government office

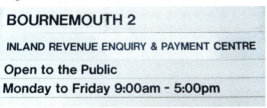

F shop

I library

C Language focus

What time is it? / What's the time?
9.00   nine o'clock / nine / nine a.m.
21.00 nine o'clock / nine / nine p.m.
20.30 eight thirty / eight thirty p.m. NOT ~~eight thirty o'clock~~

For timetables only
21.00 twenty-one hundred
20.30 twenty thirty

Time words
at 11 a.m., **at** twelve thirty
on Sunday(s), **on** weekdays
at weekends
from nine **to** twelve thirty

(It is / They are) open.   What time (does it / do they) open?
(It is / They are) closed.   What time (does it / do they) close?

1 Complete the sentences.
1 The bank is closed .... Sundays.
2 The office is open .... weekdays.
3 The post office is open .... nine to five thirty on weekdays.
4 The shop closes .... five thirty.
5 The government office is closed .... weekends.
6 The office is open from nine .... six.

2 Pair work. Look at the photos on pages 76–7.
Student A close your book. Ask about opening times.
▶ What time does the bank open on Mondays?
◀ It opens at nine.

Student B close your book. Ask about closing times.
▶ What time does the library close on Saturdays?
◀ It closes at four o'clock.

D Your country

Ask and answer about your country.
1 What time do banks open on weekdays?
2 Do any shops open twenty-four hours a day? What shops?
3 Are government offices open or closed at weekends?
4 What are the opening hours of shops on weekdays?
5 Do shops close on one day? What day?
6 Do tourist information centres open on Sundays?
7 What about bars? Libraries? Banks? What time do they open and close?

See **Extension 15** p.166

16 Asking for directions

A The Underground

**1 Look at the map.
Listen and read.** (✱ 2.31)

This is a map of the Glasgow Underground in Scotland. You're at Cessnock station on the red line, the Inner circle. The first stop is Kinning Park. The second stop is Shields Road. The third stop is West Street, and the fourth stop is Bridge Street.

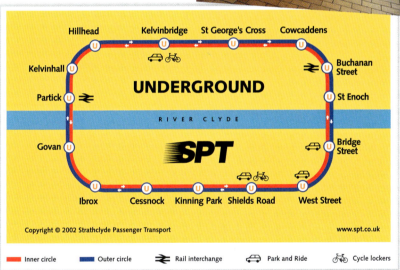

2 Listen and repeat. (✱ 2.32)

1st	2nd	3rd	4th	5th
first	second	third	fourth	fifth

6th	7th	8th	9th	10th
sixth	seventh	eighth	ninth	tenth

3 Listen. Then practise the conversation. Change the words in *italics*. (✱ 2.33)

▶ Excuse me, where's *Bridge Street*?
◀ It's the *fourth* stop.

Shields Road   *West Street*   *Kinning Park*

B Where's the bus station?

Listen. Then practise the conversations. Change the words in *italics*.

(* 2.34)

▶ Excuse me, where's the *bus station*?
◀ Sorry, I don't know. There's a map over there.
▶ Thank you.
◀ You're welcome.

post office
railway station
hospital

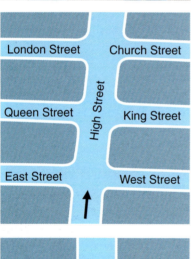

(* 2.35)

▶ Can you help me? I'm looking for *King Street*.
◀ It's the *second* street on the *right*.

first
second
third
right
left

(* 2.36)

▶ Is there a *taxi rank* near here?
◀ Yes. Go along this street. Turn *left* at the traffic lights. The taxi rank's on the *right*.
▶ OK, turn *left* at the traffic lights, and it's on the *right*. Thank you.

bus stop
telephone box
car park

C Language focus

Asking for directions
Excuse me ...
Can you help me?
Where's (*Baker Street / the bus station*)?
I'm looking for (*Baker Street / the bus station*).
Is there (*a taxi rank*) near here?
Can you give me directions (*to the bank*)?

Giving directions
It's the fourth (*stop*).
It's the second (*street*) on the (*right*).
It's on the (*right / left*).
It's at the end of (*the road*).

Go	along	Dorset Road.
	past	the bank.
	across	the bridge.
	to	the end (*of the street*).
	into	the café.

Turn	right	at the traffic lights.
	left	at the end (*of the road*).
	first right	

Match the pictures with these directions.

go across the road ☐   go past the bank ☐
go along the road ☐   go to the end of the street ☐

A

B

C

D

D Can you give me directions?

1 **Find the café on the map. Listen and draw the route on the map.** ✱ 2.37
   Complete the sentences with these words.

end   across   into   past

   1 Turn right .... the High Street.
   2 Go .... the town hall.
   3 There's a park at the .... of the High Street.
   4 Go .... the bridge.

2 **Listen. Where is Bob?** ✱ 2.38

3 **Listen again. Tick (✓) the correct answers.**
   1 Bob (☐ has   ☐ hasn't) got Tim's address.
   2 Tim lives at number (☐ 50   ☐ 15).
   3 Tim's flat is on the (☐ first   ☐ fifth) floor.

   Draw the route to Tim's flat.

4 **Suzy works at the town hall. Listen and circle the places you hear.** ✱ 2.39

5 **In pairs, choose a route for Suzy.**

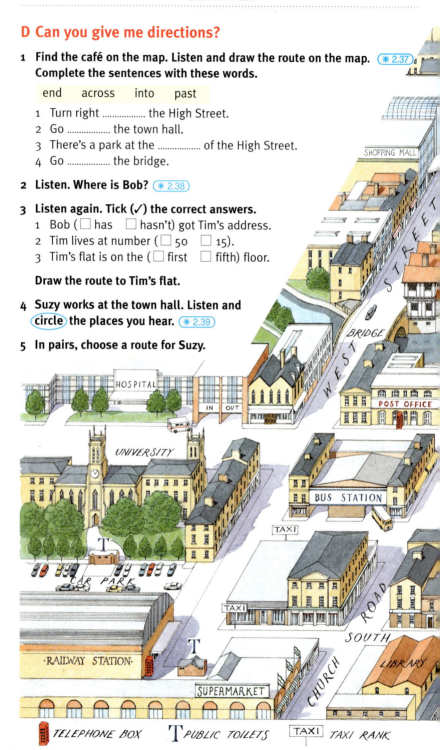

UNIT SIXTEEN 83

COMMUNICATION
Student A Look at Activity 5 on p.186.
Student B Look at Activity 15 on p.196.

E Your town

Give directions to places near the school. The other students guess the places.

See **Extension 16** p.167

17 Lifestyles

A The D.J.

1 **Listen and read the text on p.85.** ✱ 2.40

2 **Tick (✓) the true sentences.
   Correct the false sentences.**
   1 Martin works at night.
   2 He finishes work at six in the morning.
   3 He goes to bed at midnight.
   4 He gets up at one a.m.
   5 He has lunch at two thirty p.m.

3 **Answer with *Yes, he does. / No, he doesn't.***
   Does he work in the evening?
   Does he work at night?
   Does he have breakfast?
   Does he have a shower in the morning?
   Does he have lunch?

4 **Complete the sentences with these verbs.**

go   have   start   get up   finish

   He .... at one p.m.
   He .... dinner at nine or ten.
   He .... work at midnight.
   He .... work at five a.m.
   He .... to bed at six.

5 **Ask and answer about Martin with the verbs in exercise 4.**
   What time does he get up?

UNIT SEVENTEEN

'My name's Martin Hammond and I'm a D.J. I work in a club on the Costa Brava in Spain. I start work at midnight, and I finish at five a.m. I have a shower, then I go to bed at six, and I get up at one p.m. I don't have breakfast. I have lunch at two thirty. I don't work in the afternoon or evening. I have dinner at nine or ten o'clock. Then I go to work.'

B Language focus

Routines
What time do you get up? I get up at seven thirty.
What time does she go to bed? She goes to bed at ten.
What time does he finish work? He finishes work at six.
What time do they have dinner? They have dinner at eight p.m.

have
have / has breakfast / lunch / dinner
have / has a shower / bath

Questions
(What time / When) do you get up?
(What time / When) does she go to bed?
When does he work? He works from nine to five.
When do you have dinner?

1 **Make these sentences true for you.**
   I work on Saturdays. ☒
   I don't work on Saturdays.
   1 I get up at five thirty a.m. ☐
   2 I have breakfast in a café. ☐
   3 I finish work at seven p.m. ☐
   4 I have a bath in the evening. ☐
   5 I go to bed at midnight. ☐

2 **Tell your partner about your routines.**

C Working hours

1 **Listen, read, and answer.** (✱ 2.41)
   1 When does she work?
   2 When does she have lunch?
   3 When does she have a coffee break?
   4 When does she have a tea break?

2 **Listen and write the times.** (✱ 2.42)
   He gets up at ...5.30... .
   He has breakfast ....
   He works from ....
   to ....
   He has lunch from ....
   to ....
   He has dinner at ....
   He goes to bed at ....

A British worker

I work from nine to five, and I have lunch from twelve to one. I have a coffee break in the morning, and a tea break in the afternoon. I don't work at weekends.

An American worker

3 **What are the typical working hours in your country for ...**
an office worker?
a factory worker?
a waiter?
a teacher?
a shop assistant?

D TV survey

1 **Interview a partner.**

Are you a TV addict?

How many TVs are there in your home? ☐

Do you watch TV ... ?
☐ every day
☐ four or five days a week
☐ one day a week

Where do you watch TV?
☐ in the living room
☐ in my bedroom
☐ in the kitchen
☐ in a café or bar

When do you watch TV?
☐ in the mornings
☐ in the afternoons
☐ in the evenings
☐ at night

Who do you watch TV with?
☐ alone
☐ with my family
☐ with my friends
☐ with my partner

What do you watch?
☐ TV programmes
☐ videos or DVDs
☐ satellite or cable programmes

When the TV is on, do you ...?
☐ have a meal
☐ eat snacks
☐ read books and magazines
☐ talk
☐ work or study

2 **Change partners. Ask about your first partner's answers.**
Does (*she*) watch TV every day?
Who does (*she*) watch TV with?

See **Extension 17** p.168

18 Flight to Orlando

A On the plane

Katie and Tony are passengers on a flight from Manchester to Orlando. Listen, then practise the conversations.

(* 2.43)

Tony Which seat would you like? This one or that one?
Katie That one. By the window.

(* 2.44)

Attendant Would you like a drink from the bar?
Tony Yes, please. What have you got?
Attendant Wine, beer, spirits, or soft drinks.
Tony Have you got any champagne?
Attendant Yes, we have.
Tony I'd like some champagne, please.
Katie I'd like some champagne, too. We're on our honeymoon.
Attendant Oh, congratulations!

UNIT EIGHTEEN 89

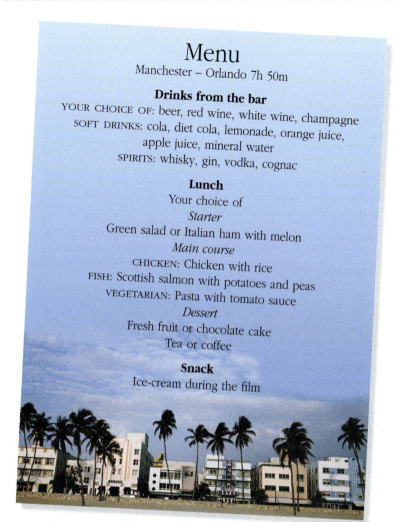

B Lunch

1 **Look at the menu. Listen to the conversation.** ✱ 2.45
2 **Listen again. Complete the table.**

	Tony	Katie
Drink with meal		
Starter		
Main course		
Dessert		
Tea or coffee		

C Language focus

I'd like ...

I	'd	like	some wine.
You	would		an ice-cream.
He			
She			
We			
They			

Questions

Would	you	like	some wine?
	he		an ice-cream?
	she		
	they		

Short answers

Yes, please.
Yes, (I) would.
No, thank you.
No, (he) wouldn't.

What would you like to drink?

Which?

Which	starter	would	you	like?
	seat		she	
	dessert		he	
			they	

Questions and offers

Use *any* with questions.
Have you got any wine? is a **question**.
The answer is *Yes, I have. / No, I haven't.*
Use *some* with offers.
Would you like some wine? is an **offer**.
The answer is *Yes, please. / No, thanks.*

this / that

I'd like this one.
That one, please.

This near, or the first one you say
That far, or the second one you say

1 Make sentences.

I / beer. / like / 'd / some.
I'd like some beer.

1 you, / No, / wouldn't. / thank / I
2 wine? / Would / some / you / like
3 like / 'd / lemonade. / some / We
4 water. / like / 'd / They / some
5 got / you / Have / champagne? / any

UNIT EIGHTEEN

2 **Complete the sentences with *this* or *that*.**

1 What's .... ?

2 Is .... your umbrella?

3 .... is my sister, Anna.

4 This is a British stamp, and .... 's an Irish stamp.

D Would you like ... ?

1 **Complete the conversation. Listen and check.** ✱ 2.46

Attendant .... you .... a newspaper?
Katie Yes, please. What .... got?
Attendant We .... got *The Times* or *USA Today*.
Katie .... like *The Times*, ...

Now make a conversation about the magazines.

2 **Complete the conversation. Listen and check.** ✱ 2.47

Attendant Would .... some tea?
Katie No, ... you got any coffee?
Attendant Yes, just .... minute.

Now make conversations about these things.

| wine | mineral water | a pillow | a blanket | cola | diet cola |

E Role play

Groups of three. Role play a conversation with the menu on p.89.

See **Extension 18** p.169

19 What can you do?

A Ability

1. **Listen and read.** (✻ 2.48)
   A She can speak five languages.
   B Help! I can't swim!
   C And the first prize is a sports car! Can you drive?
   D She can say 'Daddy'.
   E He can't sing!

   Match the sentences and the pictures.

2. **Listen and repeat.** (✻ 2.49)
   ▶ Can you whistle?
   ◀ No, I can't. Can you?
   ▶ Yes, I can. It's easy!

3. **Pair work. Practise with these words. Give true answers.**
   whistle   drive   sing   swim

UNIT NINETEEN

B Language focus

Positive and negative

I	can	swim.
You	can't	drive.
He	cannot	play the violin.
She		speak Japanese.
We		use a computer.
They		

Questions

Can	you	swim?
	he	drive?
	she	speak English?
	we	play chess?
	they	use a computer?
	I	

Short answers

Yes,	I	can.
	you	
	he	
No,	she	can't.
	we	
	they	

1 Tick (✓) the correct words.

1 They can (☐ swim   ☐ to swim).
2 She (☐ cans   ☐ can) speak Chinese.
3 We (☐ can't   ☐ don't can) drive.
4 (☐ Do you can   ☐ Can you) whistle?

2 Listen to the sounds. ✱ 2.50

A /kæn/   can   ☐
B /kən/   can   ☐
C /kɑːnt/ can't ☐

Listen to the sentences. Write A, B or C.

1 Can you swim?   ☐
2 Yes, I can.   ☐
3 I can play the guitar.   ☐
4 I can't speak Italian.   ☐
5 Can she use Microsoft Office?   ☐
6 He can't drive, but she can.   ☐ ☐

C Can you do it?

1 Interview five students in your class. Note the answers.

Can you play ...

the piano   the guitar
the saxophone

Can you speak ...

Spanish   German   French

Can you play ...

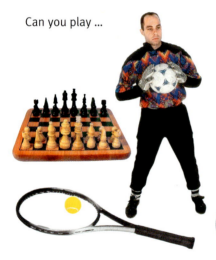

chess   tennis   football

Can you use ...

a word processor   a web browser
an e-mail program

2 Ask your partner questions.
▶ Can (*Maria*) play the piano?
◀ Yes, (*she*) can. / No, (*she*) can't. / I don't know.

3 Make sentences about the class.
(*Maria*) can play the guitar.
(*Paul*) can't speak French.

D Skills

Listen and complete the form for Kevin. (✱ 2.51)

Employment Agency
Registration form

PAGE 3
Section B: Skills
1 Can you drive? ☐ Yes ☐ No
2 Have you got an HGV licence? ☐ Yes ☐ No
3 Can you speak a foreign language? ☐ Yes ☐ No
  Which language(s) can you speak?

  [   ]

  [   ]

Computer skills
4 Can you type? ☐ Yes ☐ No
5 Can you use …? ☐ a PC
  ☐ a word-processor (e.g. Microsoft Word)
  ☐ a spreadsheet (e.g. Microsoft Excel)

E What can you do in English?

Pair work.

A ask B
- Can you say the alphabet in English?
- Can you name five things in your classroom?
- Can you sing a song in English?
- Can you spell your teacher's name?
- Can you give directions from the school to a car park?

B ask A
- Can you say the days of the week?
- Can you name eight colours?
- Can you count from eleven to twenty in English?
- Can you describe your room at home?
- Can you talk about your routines?

Which things are easy for you? Which things are difficult?

See **Extension 19** p.170

20 Appointments

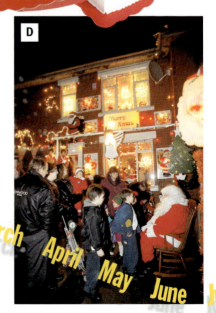

Valentine

January February March April May June

UNIT TWENTY 97

A Months and dates

1 **Match the days and the pictures.**
New Year's Day ☐   American Independence Day ☐
Valentine's Day ☐   Christmas Day ☐

2 **Match the dates and the pictures.**
4th July ☐   1st January ☐   25th December ☐   14th February ☐

Then listen and check. (✻ 2.52)
Write 21st May / May 21st / 21 May / May 21
Say the twenty-first of May / May the twenty-first

3 **Listen and repeat the months of the year.** (✻ 2.53)

4 **Practise months and dates. Listen and repeat.** (✻ 2.54)

11th – eleventh   12th – twelfth   13th – thirteenth
15th – fifteenth   20th – twentieth   22nd – twenty-second
23rd – twenty-third   31st – thirty-first

Say aloud.
14th 16th 17th 18th 19th
21st 24th 25th 26th
27th 28th 29th 30th

Write sentences for the twelve months.
January is the first month.
November May March September June October
February December April August July

What's the date today? What's the date tomorrow?

B Important dates

1 **Ask about birthdays.**
▶ When's your birthday?
◀ My birthday's (*the 3rd of February*).
▶ When's your father's birthday?
◀ His birthday's (*the 20th of August*).

2 **Has any student in your class got the same birthday as you, or one of your family?**

3 **What are three important dates in your country?**

C Making an appointment

1 **Listen. What's the day and date today?**

(✱ 2.55)
Receptionist Can I help you?
Mr Benson Yes. Can I make an appointment with Dr Wilson, please?
Receptionist What's your name?
Mr Benson Matthew Benson.

(✱ 2.56)
Receptionist How about Monday the 27th of July?
Mr Benson Oh, dear. Can I see her today?
Receptionist I'm sorry. She's very busy today.
Mr Benson Is she free tomorrow?
Receptionist Thursday? Yes. Morning or afternoon?
Mr Benson Can I see her in the evening?
Receptionist No, I'm afraid you can't. She finishes at five o'clock.

(✱ 2.57)
Mr Benson OK. How about tomorrow morning?
Receptionist What time?
Mr Benson Early. Eight thirty or nine?
Receptionist No, I'm sorry. She's got appointments then.
Is eleven o'clock OK?
Mr Benson All right.
Receptionist Fine. Thursday the 23rd of July at eleven o'clock.
Mr Benson Thank you.

UNIT TWENTY

2 **Practise the conversation. Change the days, dates, and times.**

3 **Listen to the conversations. Find the people in the picture.**

	Name	Date	Time
✱ 2.58	Mrs Adams		
✱ 2.59	Darren Morley		
✱ 2.60	Isobel Patton		
✱ 2.61	Mr Atkins		

4 **Listen again. When are their appointments? Note the dates and times.**

JULY						
Mon	Tue	Wed	Thur	Fri	Sat	Sun
		1	2	3	4	5
6	7	8	9	10	11	12
13	14	15	16	17	18	19
20	21	22	23	24	25	26
27	28	29	30	31		

D Language focus

in	January / the evening / 2005
on	Friday / the 13th / 13th June
at	six o'clock / 4.30 / 21.00

Remember write *13th June*, say *the* 13th *of* June
today   this week   this month
tomorrow   next week   next month

***can* for requests**
Can I make an appointment?
Can I see her tomorrow?
Can I make an appointment for July 2nd?
No, I'm sorry. / No, I'm afraid you can't.

Suggestions
How about (*Thursday morning*)?
Is (*eight thirty*) OK?

Complete the sentences with *in*, *on*, or *at*.
1 I'd like an appointment .... the afternoon.
2 She hasn't got any appointments .... Tuesday.
3 Can I see her .... nine o'clock?
4 She starts work .... nine thirty.
5 He's free .... 31st January.
6 My birthday's .... February.

COMMUNICATION

Student A Look at Activity 6 on p.187.
Student B Look at Activity 16 on p.197.

E Early or late?

Answer about your country.
1 People are (☐ late ☐ on time ☐ early) for appointments.
2 Is 30 minutes late OK?
   ☐ yes   ☐ no   ☐ sometimes
3 How late are people for appointments?
   ☐ 5 minutes   ☐ 10 minutes   ☐ 30 minutes
   ☐ more than thirty minutes
4 Are people late for these appointments? Put (✓) for yes, (✗) for no.
   ☐ trains   ☐ business meetings   ☐ doctors   ☐ dentists
   ☐ school / college   ☐ dinner with friends   ☐ parties

See **Extension 20** p.171

21 What's she doing?

A Conversation

Listen and practise. ✹ 2.62

Man	Can I speak to Anna, please?
Woman	No, I'm sorry. She isn't here at the moment.
Man	Oh? What's she doing?
Woman	She's having lunch.

UNIT TWENTY-ONE

B What are they doing?

1 **Match the sentences and the pictures.
 Complete with *He's ...* , *She's ...* or *They're ...* .**

 1 .... having a shower. ☐
 2 .... sleeping. ☐
 3 .... sitting on a plane. ☐
 4 .... watching TV. ☐
 5 .... phoning a friend. ☐
 6 .... shopping. ☐

2 **Ask and answer.**

 Picture B
 ▶ What's he doing?
 ◀ He's phoning a friend.

C Language focus

The present continuous
Positive and negative

I	'm	watching TV.
	am	having a shower.
	'm not	listening.
You	're	shopping.
We	are	phoning her.
They	aren't	sleeping.
He	's	
She	is	
	isn't	

Questions

Are	you	watching TV?
	we	having a shower?
	they	shopping?
		working?
Is	he	
	she	

Short answers

Yes,	I am.
No,	I'm not.
Yes,	we are.
No,	they aren't.
Yes,	he is.
No,	she isn't.

What are you doing?   **Who** is she phoning?

do / doing   have / having   stop / stopping

Why (can't he help her)?   **Because** (he's having a shower).

1 Make sentences.

they / plane? / on / Are / sitting / a
Are they sitting on a plane?
1 sister. / She / her / 's / phoning
2 a / He / bath. / having / isn't
3 film. / watching / We / old / an / 're
4 you / classroom? / Are / sitting / a / in
5 today. / 'm / working / I / not

2 Spelling. Rewrite these verbs with -ing.

phone	....	stop	....
sleep	....	do	....
sit	....	help	....
use	....	video	....
take off	....	play	....
talk	....	make	....
watch	....		

D She's working late

Tracy's favourite TV programme is *Neighbours*. It's on TV at the moment. She can't watch it because she's working late at the office.

1 **Listen to her phone conversations. Her family and friends can't help her. Why not? Write the reasons next to the names.**

	Name	Reason
✳ 2.63	Tracy's dad	
✳ 2.64	Tracy's mum	
✳ 2.65	Dave	
✳ 2.66	Jordan and Alice	
✳ 2.67	Ellen	

2 True (✓) or false (✗)?

1 Her dad can video the programme.
2 Her mum isn't shopping.
3 Pete is sleeping.
4 The plane is taking off.
5 Ellen's got a videotape.

3 Practise questions and answers.

Who's doing it?
▶ Who's having a shower?
◀ Tracy's dad is having a shower.

What are they doing?
▶ What's her dad doing?
◀ He's having a shower.

Why not?
▶ Why can't her dad help her?
◀ Because he's having a shower.

E Your friends and family

Ask and answer about your friends and family.
What are they doing now?
▶ What's your (*boyfriend*) doing now?
◀ He's having dinner at home.
▶ What's your (*sister*) doing now?
◀ I don't know.

- My brother's working.
- My sister's playing tennis.
- I'm studying English at the moment.
- My mother's using the Internet.
- My father's reading a book.

COMMUNICATION
Student A Look at Activity 7 on p.188.
Student B Look at Activity 17 on p.198.

See **Extension 21** p.172

22 Plans

A I'm going out

1 **Listen.** (✱ 2.68)

Debbie's a hairdresser. She's cutting Gemma's hair.

Debbie What are you doing on Saturday?
Gemma I'm going out.
Debbie Where are you going?
Gemma I'm going to a club. What are you doing?
Debbie I'm staying in. I haven't got any money.

Practise the conversation.

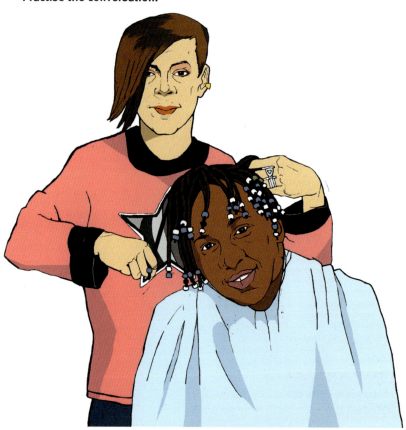

2 **Ask and answer about different days. Give true answers.**
   ► What are you doing (*tomorrow* / *on Sunday* / *next weekend*)?
   ◄ I'm staying in. / I'm going to (*the cinema*). / I don't know. I haven't got any plans.

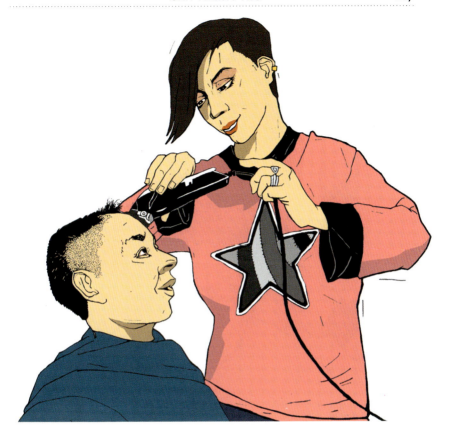

B Holiday plans

1 **Complete the conversation with these answers.**

> August.   Yes, I'm going to Italy.   Rimini's very popular.   Rimini.

Debbie Are you going on holiday this year?
Mark ……………………………………… .
Debbie Really? Where to?
Mark ……………………………………… .
Debbie That's nice.
Mark ……………………………………… .
Debbie Yes, I know. When are you going?
Mark ……………………………………… .
Debbie Oh, really? Italy's lovely in August. Very hot.

Now listen and check. (✻ 2.69)

2 **Listen and repeat Debbie's responses.** (✻ 2.70)
Really?   That's nice.   Yes, I know.   Oh, really?

3 **Role play a conversation about holidays.**

C Sympathetic listening

1 **Listen and match.** (✱ 2.71)

Mrs Baxter
1 She's having an operation on Monday.
2 I'm taking him to the vet this afternoon.
3 He's got the flu.
4 He's sneezing all the time.

Debbie
A Oh, dear.
B That's awful.
C Oh, I am sorry.
D Oh, no.

2 **Who is Mrs Baxter talking about? Look at the sentences in exercise 1. Write** B (Mr Baxter), L (Mrs Lester), D (her dog).

3 **Complete the questions with** *he*, *she*, **or** *it*.
Then ask and answer.
1 When is .... having an operation?
2 When is she taking .... to the vet?
3 When is .... seeing the doctor?

4 **Listen again. Reply for Debbie when you hear 'ting!'.** (✱ 2.72)

D Language focus

The present continuous for future plans

I	'm	going out	on Sunday.
	'm not	staying at home	tomorrow.
He	's	going on holiday	this evening.
She	isn't		next week.
We	're		
You	aren't		
They			

What	are you	doing	tomorrow?
	is she		this evening?
	am I		on Sunday?
Where	is he	going	next week?
	are they		
	are we		

Sympathetic listening
That's nice.   Really?   Oh, really?   Yes, I know.
Oh, dear.   I am sorry.   Oh, no.   That's awful.

Make sentences.

(−) They / not / go / Spain / this summer.
They aren't going to Spain this summer.

1 (?) you / stay / at home / this evening?
2 (+) She / see / her boyfriend / tonight.
3 (−) I / not go / work / tomorrow.
4 (+) They / meet / friends / next Saturday.
5 (−) We / not / go out / on Sunday.
6 (?) he / go / the cinema / on Saturday?

E Diary

1 **Look at the diary. Make sentences.**

He's seeing the doctor on Monday at 10.30.

2 **Write notes for your diary for next week.**

3 **Interview a partner about his or her diary. Respond sympathetically.**

That's nice.   Oh, dear.   Oh, really?

See **Extension 22** p.173

23 An evening out

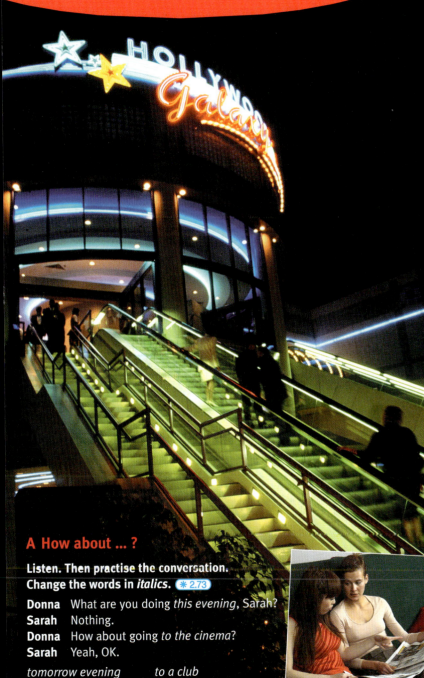

A How about ... ?

**Listen. Then practise the conversation.
Change the words in *italics*.** ✱ 2.73

Donna What are you doing *this evening*, Sarah?
Sarah Nothing.
Donna How about going *to the cinema*?
Sarah Yeah, OK.

tomorrow evening   *to a club*
on Saturday night   *for a drink*
next Sunday   *for a pizza*

B Let's go

Listen. Then practise the conversation. Change the words in *italics*.

✱ 2.74

Sarah	What's on?
Donna	*Paranoia*. At the Odeon.
Sarah	Who's in it?
Donna	*Catherine Grant*.
Sarah	Oh, I like *her*. What time?
Donna	*7.30* or *9.45*.
Sarah	Let's go to the *7.30*.

ODEON MULTIPLEX
Harbourside Shopping Village, Cranley

SCREEN 1
STAR EXPLORER
with Patrick Dylan
4.10   6.55   8.40   10.35

SCREEN 2
SUMMER OF 99
with Cherie Lee
5.20   7.50   10.20

SCREEN 3
PARANOIA
with Catherine Grant
4.15   7.30   9.45

SCREEN 4
LOVE LETTERS
with Jack Douglas & Lucy Ford
4.25   7.00   9.35

C Let's get some nachos

Listen. Then practise the conversation. Change the words in *italics*.

ODEON MULTIPLEX
POPCORN 2.90
NACHOS 2.60
FRENCH FRIES 2.30
MILK SHAKE 1.75
COLA 1.80
LEMONADE 1.80

✱ 2.75

Donna	Let's get some *nachos*.
Sarah	Not for me, thanks. I don't like *nachos*.
Donna	What about a *milk shake*, then?
Sarah	No, I'm on a diet.
Donna	Oh, well. It's *7.30*. Let's go in.

D Language focus

Suggestions

| How | about | some popcorn? |
| What | | a milk shake? |

How	about	going	to the cinema?
What			for a drink?
		seeing a film?	

| Let's | get some popcorn. |
| | go in. |

like, don't like

I	like	him.
You	don't like	her.
We		them.
They		Patrick Dylan.
He	likes	popcorn.
She	doesn't like	cola.

Questions

Do	you	like	him?
	we		her?
	they		them?
	I		Patrick Dylan?
Does	he		popcorn?
	she		cola?

Short answers

Yes, (I) do. / No, (we) don't.
Yes, (he) does. / No, (she) doesn't.

1 Choose the correct word.

1 What about (☐ go ☐ to go ☐ going) for a drink?
2 Let's (☐ get ☐ to get ☐ getting) some French fries.
3 He (☐ doesn't ☐ don't) like her.
4 Does she (☐ likes ☐ like) Patrick Dylan?

2 Listen and answer.

- ✱ 2.76 Does she like him?
- ✱ 2.77 Does she like him?
  Does she like her?
- ✱ 2.78 Does he like popcorn?
- ✱ 2.79 Does she like the music?
- ✱ 2.80 Does he like Maria?

E What do you like?

1 Label the pictures with these words.

opera   ballet   theatre   football   classical music   rock music

A .... B .... C ....

D .... E .... F ....

2 Pair work. Ask and answer.
- ▶ Do you like (*classical music*)?
- ◀ Yes, I do. / No, I don't.

3 Change partners. Ask about your first partner.
- ▶ Does (she / he) like (*football*)?
- ◀ Yes, (she) does. / No, (he) doesn't.

F What's on in your town?

1 What's on this week? Write true sentences.

	What?	*Where?*	*When?*
There's	a new film	at the cinema	this week.
	a rock concert	at the theatre	at 8 o'clock tonight.
	a football match	at the stadium	on Saturday.
	a ballet	at the concert hall	
	a play	at the town hall	
	an opera	in London	

2 Pair work. Look at your partner's sentences. Ask for more information.

Which (*opera / ballet / play*) is it?
Who's playing? (*football match / rock concert*)
What are they playing? (*classical concert*)

3 Role play a conversation.

▶ (How / What) about seeing (*Hamlet*) at the (*National Theatre*)?
◀ Yes, OK. When?
▶ Let's go on (*Friday*).
◀ No, sorry, I can't. I'm busy on (*Friday*).
▶ How about (*Saturday*)?
◀ Yes, that's OK.

4 Group work. Find a day and time when your group can meet. Make suggestions for an activity, e.g. go for a pizza, see a film or go to a concert or sports match.

See **Extension 23** p.174

24 Likes and dislikes

A *like*, *love*, and *hate*

1 **Look at the table. Listen and repeat.** ✱ 2.81
2 **Complete the table.**

✓✓	✓	–	✗	✗✗
I love it.	I like it.	It's OK.	I don't like it.	I hate it.
He *loves it*.	He	It's OK.	She	He ....

UNIT TWENTY-FOUR 117

B Do you like this music?

1 **Listen to the five pieces of music. Stop after each piece of music. Ask and answer.** (✱ 2.82 - 2.86)
   ▶ Do you like it?
   ◀ Yes, I love it. / Yes, I like it. / It's OK. / No, I don't like it. / No, I hate it. What about you?
   ▶ I like it.

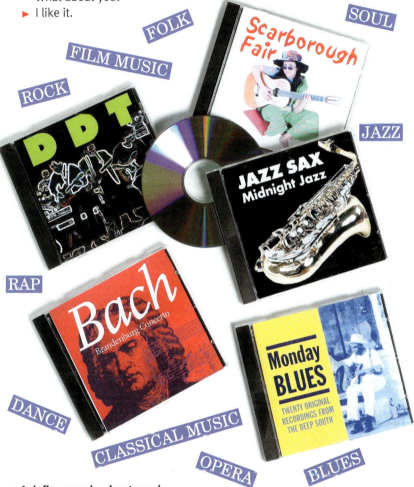

2 **Ask five people about music.**
   ▶ Do you like (*classical music*)?
   ◀ Yes, I do. / No, I don't. / I love it. / I hate it. / It's OK.
   ▶ Which (*singers / groups / composers*) do you like?
   ◀ I like (*Jennifer Lopez / The Beatles / Beethoven*).

3 **Ask and answer about people in your class.**
   ▶ Does (*Maria*) like dance music?
   ◀ Yes, (*she*) does. / No, (*she*) doesn't. / (*She*) loves it. / (*She*) hates it.

C What do you like doing?

1 Interview a partner.

QUESTIONNAIRE

Tick or cross.
✓ ✓ I love it.   ✓ I like it.
✗ I don't like it.   ✗ ✗ I hate it.

Taking exercise
Do you like … ?
swimming ☐
running ☐
walking ☐
playing tennis ☐
What other things do you like doing?
....

Going out
Do you like … ?
shopping ☐
eating out ☐
going to the cinema ☐
dancing ☐
going out with friends ☐
What other things do you like doing?
....

Staying in
Do you like … ?
cleaning the house ☐
cooking ☐
watching TV ☐
reading ☐
surfing the Internet ☐
listening to music ☐
What other things do you like doing?
....

2 Change partners. Ask about your first partner's answers.

▶ Does (she) like swimming?
◀ Yes, she does. / No, she doesn't. / She loves it. / She hates it.

D Language focus

Likes and dislikes

Do	you	like	rock music?
Does	she		swimming?

What do you like doing?

I	love	classical music.
You	like	Beethoven.
We	don't like	The Beatles.
They	hate	swimming.
He	loves	dancing.
She	likes	playing tennis.
	doesn't like	watching TV.
	hates	

From a survey in British schools

Boys like ...

playing football	78%
swimming	40%
playing basketball	39%
doing martial arts	22%
playing tennis	21%

Girls like ...

dancing	72%
playing netball	53%
swimming	50%
doing gymnastics	29%
playing tennis	23%

1 **Read the results of the survey. Make five sentences.**
   Twenty-nine per cent of girls like doing gymnastics.

2 **What do boys and girls like doing in your country? Make five sentences.**

3 **Which activities in the survey are popular in your class? Make a chart.**

4 **Make sentences about your family and friends.**
   My son loves watching Disney cartoons.
   My sister doesn't like dogs.
   My parents like going out in their car on Sundays.

COMMUNICATION

Choose one student (Student A).
Student A Look at Activity 8 on p.189. Don't tell anyone!
All the other students Look at Activity 18 on p.199.

See **Extension 24** p.175

25 What are you going to do?

A Titanic

1 **Match the sentences and the pictures.**
   A The ship's going to sink.
   B They're going to fall in love.
   C He's going to die.
   D They're going to jump.
   E *Titanic* is my favourite film.
   F They aren't going to get married.

2 **Listen to the conversations and check.**
   ✳ 2.87 - 2.92

UNIT TWENTY-FIVE

5

6

B What's going to happen?

Make sentences about the pictures. Use words from the box.

It's going to rain.

| rain | have a shower | be late | jump | have a baby | get married |

Listen and check. ✱ 2.93

C Language focus

going to for the future

(*it*) + *going to* + verb

It	's	going to	rain.
	isn't		

going to + be + adjective

It	's	going to	be	late.
He	is			hot.
She	isn't			cold.
We	're			
You	are			
They	aren't			
I	'm			
	'm not			

What	are	you	going to	do?
	is	she		

(*I*) + *going to* + verb

I	'm	going to	have a baby.
	'm not		jump.
You	're		win the lottery.
We	aren't		
They			
He	's		
She	isn't		

Choose the correct word.
1 Who's going (☐ win ☐ to win) the Academy Award this year?
2 Where are you (☐ going ☐ go) to go this evening?
3 Is it going (☐ raining ☐ to rain)?
4 What are you going (☐ buy ☐ to buy) for her birthday?

COMMUNICATION
Student A Look at Activity 9 on p.190.
Student B Look at Activity 19 on p.200.

D What are you going to do?

1 **Imagine. You are the winner of the lottery. Answer the questions.**

   1 Are you going to give all the money to charity?
   2 Are you going to buy a fast car?
   3 Are you going to leave your job / leave school?
   4 Are you going to give money to your family?
   5 Are you going to buy a lottery ticket next week?

2 **Look at the lottery ticket. Choose a line of numbers, A, B, or C. Listen.** ✱ 2.94

   Listen to the numbers again.
   ✱ 2.95
   Which students are the winners?

3 **Ask the winners questions about the money.**

   ▶ Are you going to buy a new house?
   ◀ Yes, I am. / No, I'm not.

E Talk about your future

Claire
I'm going to go to university.
I'm going to get a degree.
I'm going to get a good job.
I'm going to fall in love.
I'm going to get married.
I'm going to have three children.

Tessa
I'm going to be a film star.
I'm going to be famous.
I'm going to live in Hollywood.
I'm not going to fall in love.
I'm not going to get married.
I'm not going to have any children.

1 Ask and answer about Claire and Tessa.

► Is (*Tessa*) going to get married?
◄ No, she isn't. / Yes, she is.
► Who's going to get married?
◄ (*Claire*)'s going to get married.

2 Talk about your future. Ask about your partner's future.

See **Extension 25** p.176

26 Where was it?

A The lottery ticket

1 **Read and listen.** ✱ 3.02

2 **Choose the correct word.**
   1 There (☐ was ☐ wasn't) a lottery winner last week.
   2 The prize (☐ is ☐ isn't) twenty million this week.
   3 The ticket (☐ is ☐ isn't) in the pocket of her jeans.
   4 Her jeans (☐ were ☐ weren't) in the bedroom yesterday.
   5 The jeans (☐ are ☐ aren't) in the shop now.
   6 The shop (☐ is ☐ isn't) closed.

3 **What are they going to do? Choose an answer.**
   • They're going to buy the jeans.
   • They aren't going to buy the jeans.
   • They're going to ask for the ticket.
   • They're going to take the ticket from the pocket.

4 **Act out the story.**

B Pronunciation

Listen and repeat. (* 3.03)

/wəz/ and /wə/ = **unstressed**

1. /wəz/ I was tired yesterday.
2. /wəz/ She was at home last Sunday.
3. /wə/ We were in Spain last year.
4. /wə/ You were in Paris last weekend.
5. /wəz/ Was she there?
6. /wə/ Were they late?

/wɒz/ and /wɜː/ = **stressed**

7. /wɒz/ Yes, she was.
8. /wɒz/ Yes, I was.
9. /wɜː/ Yes, we were.
10. /wɜː/ Yes, you were.

C Language focus

The past simple, *to be*
It isn't here now. It was here yesterday.
They aren't here now. They were here yesterday.

Positive and negative

I	was	there.
She	wasn't	here.
He		at home.
It		in Japan.
We	were	busy.
You	weren't	tired.
They		

Questions

Were	you	there?
	we	here?
	they	at home?
Was	he	in Japan?
	she	busy?

Short answers

Yes, (we) were.
No, (they) weren't.

Yes, (she) was.
No, (I) wasn't.

Time words

present	today	this (*week*)	this (*year*)
past	yesterday	last (*week*)	last (*year*)
future	tomorrow	next (*week*)	next (*year*)

Make sentences about today and yesterday.

Today it's hot. Yesterday it was cold.

	Today	Yesterday
1	It / hot.	It / cold.
2	I / at school.	I / not at school.
3	She / happy.	She / unhappy.
4	They / busy.	They / not busy.
5	He / tired.	He / busy.
6	We / at school.	We / at home.

D Where was it?

1 **Listen to the conversations.**

A I can't find my *pen*!
B Here it is.
A Thanks! Where was it?
B It was *under the newspaper*.

A I can't find my *keys*!
B Here they are.
A Thanks! Where were they?
B They were *on the shelf*.

2 **Make conversations. Change the words in *italics*.**

map   in the wastebin   glasses   in the drawer
shoes   under the bed   mobile phone   on the table

COMMUNICATION

Student A Look at Activity 10 on p.191.
Student B Look at Activity 20 on p.201.

E Where were you yesterday?

1 **Make five true sentences about yesterday. Use *was* or *wasn't*. Use words from the box.**

at home   I wasn't at home yesterday.

at home	busy	tired	at work	at school
here	angry	in a restaurant	at the cinema	with friends
in a club	late for (*an appointment*)			

2 **Interview another student.**

▶ Were you (*busy*) yesterday?
◀ Yes, I was. / No, I wasn't.
▶ Where were you (*yesterday*)?
◀ I was (*at home*).

Ask and answer about
last week   last Sunday   last Friday night

See **Extension 26** p.177

27 The weather

A Weather

1 **Listen and repeat.** (✱ 3.06)

What's the weather like?
It's cloudy.   It's sunny.   It's raining.   It's snowing.
It's hot.   It's cold.   It's windy.

Match the words and the symbols.

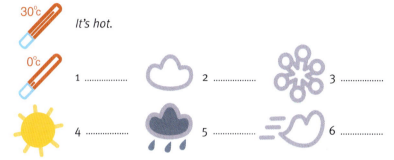

It's hot.

1 ....   2 ....   3 ....
4 ....   5 ....   6 ....

2 **Describe the weather in the pictures.**

3 **Talk about the weather.** (✱ 3.07)

▶ What's the weather like today?
◀ It's cold and cloudy.
▶ What was the weather like yesterday?
◀ It was raining. It wasn't cold.

4 **Pair work. Ask and answer about yesterday's weather.**

▶ What was the weather like in Sydney?
◀ It was hot and sunny.

WEATHER AROUND THE WORLD

Yesterday at 12 noon

London	R	14
Madrid	C	17
Moscow	Sn	−4
New York	Sn	0
Paris	C	16
Rome	S	20
Cape Town	S	32
Tokyo	R	22

S – sunny, Sn – snowing,
R – raining, C – cloudy
Temperature in degrees Celsius.

B Meeting a stranger

Driver Ms Robertson?
Woman Yes?
Driver I'm your driver. From Airport Limos.
Woman Thanks for meeting me.
Driver How was your flight?
Woman Oh, not bad.
Driver How long was it?
Woman Eleven hours. But there were some good films on the plane.
Driver OK. What was the weather like in England?
Woman It was cold and cloudy in London.
Driver Well, it's hot and sunny here in L.A. The car's outside. Let me take your bag. It's this way …

1 **Listen. Ask and answer.** ✱ 3.08
  1 Where is Ms Robertson now?
  2 How long was her flight?
  3 What was was the weather like in England?
  4 What is the weather like in Los Angeles?

UNIT TWENTY-SEVEN   133

Chauffeur – from V.I.P. Cars
Train journey? Three hours.
A restaurant? A buffet.
Food? OK.
Weather/Paris? Hot and sunny.
Cold and cloudy – London

2 **Listen and look at the notes.** (✱ 3.09)
3 **Role play the conversation.**

C Language focus

| How | was | the journey?
the flight?
the food?
the weather? | What | was | the weather like?
the flight
the journey
the food |

| awful | OK | not bad | good | very good |

| How long | was | the flight?
the journey? | Eight hours.
Thirty minutes. |

| There | was
wasn't
were
weren't | a buffet.
a restaurant.
some good films.
any films. |

Make sentences.
flight? / your / How / was
How was your flight?

1 long / How / journey? / your / was
2 plane. / weren't / the / There / on / films / any
3 wasn't / food / The / bad.
4 train. / There / buffet / on / was / the / a
5 weather / the / like? / was / What

UNIT TWENTY-SEVEN

D Holidays

1 Match the seasons and pictures. Are they the same in your country?

Seasons in Britain

☐ winter	December 21st – March 20th
☐ spring	March 21st – June 20th
☐ summer	June 21st – September 20th
☐ autumn (UK) / fall (USA)	September 21st – December 20th

2 Complete the sentences with *was* or *were*.

My last holiday (1)............. in the summer. I (2)................ in Cornwall in England with some friends. We (3)................ camping. The weather (4)................ wonderful. We (5)................ on the beach every day. The food (6)................ very good. There (7)................ a good fish restaurant near the campsite, and there (8)................ three pubs in the village.

Now listen and check. (✳ 3.10)

3 Talk about your last holiday.

- When was your last holiday?
  - ☐ in the (*spring*)
  - ☐ last (*August*)
  - ☐ last (*month*)
- Were you ... ?
  - ☐ alone
  - ☐ with a friend / friends
  - ☐ with your family
- Where were you?
  - ☐ in the mountains
  - ☐ on the beach
  - ☐ in a city
  - ☐ in the country
- Were you ... ?
  - ☐ in a hotel
  - ☐ camping
  - ☐ in a villa
  - ☐ in an apartment
- What was the weather like?
- How was the food?

E Writing

Write about your last holiday.

See **Extension 27** p.178

28 What did you have?

A We ask the questions ...

1 Read the text.

WE ASK THE QUESTIONS ...
THE 'Y' MAGAZINE INTERVIEW

This month, Darren O'Brien, lead singer of rock group 'Mirage'.

Darren, did you have a happy childhood?
Yeah. I did. I've got two brothers, and my mum and dad had a house in the country. We had a great time. We had big birthday parties.
Did you have singing lessons?
No, I didn't. I had piano lessons for a year, but I wasn't very good.
What did you have for your last birthday?
I had a CD from my girlfriend, a pair of socks from my mum, a bottle of aftershave from my dad. Oh, and a new Jaguar sports car from my manager.
When did you last have a haircut?
I had a haircut last month. Why?
No reason. What did you do yesterday?
I had a shower about eleven o'clock. Then I had lunch at three o'clock, and then dinner at ... mmm ... ten o'clock. It was a hard day. I had a lot of work yesterday.

A lot of work?
Were you in the recording studio?
No. I had a meeting with my bank manager. Then I had a meeting with my accountant and a meeting with my lawyer.
OK. Darren, what did you have for breakfast this morning?
That's a stupid question. I like white coffee and toast for my breakfast. This morning, I didn't have any milk in the fridge, and I didn't have any bread, so I just had black coffee and a cigarette.
What time did you have breakfast?
Oh, early. I had breakfast at eleven thirty.
And that's early?
That's early for me.
Thanks, Darren. Good luck with your new record.
Cheers, mate. Nice to meet you.

2 Listen and read. (✱ 3.11)

3 Make true sentences about Darren.

| Darren | had
didn't have | an unhappy childhood.
a happy childhood.
piano lessons.
singing lessons.
a Jaguar for his birthday.
a shower yesterday.
a haircut yesterday.
eggs for breakfast. |

4 **Answer with *Yes, he did. / No, he didn't.***
   1 Did his parents have a house in the country?
   2 Did he have a pair of socks for his birthday?
   3 Did he have birthday parties when he was a child?
   4 Did he have toast for breakfast this morning?
   5 Did he have breakfast at nine thirty?

5 **Ask and answer.**
   1 What did he have for his last birthday?
   2 Who did he have meetings with yesterday?
   3 What did he have for breakfast this morning?

B Mealtimes

Listen to the descriptions.
Match them to the photos.
Guess the countries.

	Photo	Country
✳ 3.12		
✳ 3.13		
✳ 3.14		
✳ 3.15		

C Language focus

The past simple
Positive and negative

I	had	dinner.
You	didn't have	a meeting.
He		toast for breakfast.
She		a shower yesterday.
We		a great time.
They		

Questions

Did	you	have	lunch	yesterday?
	we		dinner	last night?
	they		a meeting	
	he			
	she			
	I			

Short answers

Yes, (I) did.
Yes, (she) did.
No, (we) didn't.
No, (he) didn't.

Wh- questions

What did you have for lunch?
Where did he have lunch?
Who did they have lunch with?
When did she have lunch?

---

1 Interview your partner.

A General questions

How many meals do you have a day?
Do you have snacks between meals?
What do you have between meals?
☐ tea ☐ coffee ☐ chocolate
☐ biscuits ☐ fruit
☐ sweets ☐ crisps
☐ nuts ☐ cakes

B Yesterday morning

Think about yesterday.
What did you have for breakfast?
Did you have anything to drink between breakfast and lunch?
What did you have?
Did you have anything to eat between breakfast and lunch?
What did you have?

C Yesterday afternoon

When did you have lunch?
Where did you have lunch?
Who did you have lunch with?
What did you have for lunch?

2 Ask about yesterday evening.

D Parties

In your country ...
When do you have parties in your country?
Do you have parties for children's birthdays?
Do you have parties for adults' birthdays?
Do you have parties for New Year?
Do you have 'house-warming' parties (when people move to a new home)?
Do you have parties when people leave their jobs?

At your last party ...
Did you have any presents?
Did you have any special food?
What drinks did you have?
Did you have any music?
Who were the guests?
How many guests were there?

See **Extension 28** p.179

29 What did you do?

A Questions about the past

1 Tick (✓) the boxes.

1 Did you go shopping last weekend?
   ☐ Yes, I did.   ☐ No, I didn't.
2 Did you buy anything last Saturday?
   ☐ Yes, I did.   ☐ No, I didn't.
3 Did you have dinner at home last night?
   ☐ Yes, I did.   ☐ No, I didn't.
4 Did you go out last night?
   ☐ Yes, I did.   ☐ No, I didn't.
5 Did you see a film last weekend?
   ☐ Yes, I did.   ☐ No, I didn't.
6 Did you get any letters yesterday?
   ☐ Yes, I did.   ☐ No, I didn't.

2 Now you can ask questions in the past, and you can give short answers. Practise in pairs. Ask and answer the questions.

B At the supermarket

1 **Listen to five conversations. Find the people A to J in the picture.**

2 **Write the past tense.**

Present	have	go	see	buy	get
Past					

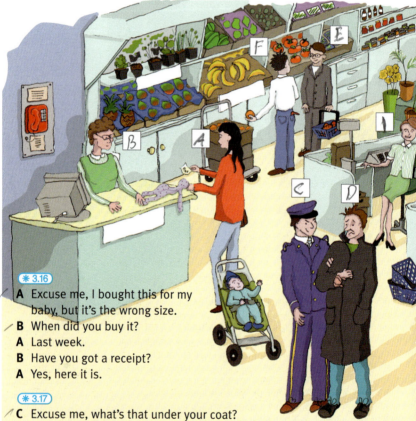

✱ 3.16
- **A** Excuse me, I bought this for my baby, but it's the wrong size.
- **B** When did you buy it?
- **A** Last week.
- **B** Have you got a receipt?
- **A** Yes, here it is.

✱ 3.17
- **C** Excuse me, what's that under your coat?
- **D** It's a frozen chicken.
- **C** Did you buy it here?
- **D** No, I didn't. I bought it from a man in the street.

✱ 3.18
- **E** Excuse me, I'm looking for organic apples.
- **F** We don't sell them.
- **E** Yes, you do. You had some yesterday. I saw them. But they aren't there now.
- **F** Oh, sorry. I'm new here.

3 Make sentences.
1 Gary. / cinema / She / the / went / to / with
2 she / it ?/ buy / did / When
3 under / He / chicken / had / his / frozen / a / coat.
4 yesterday. / the / saw / apples / He / organic
5 the / get / bread. / didn't / He

4 Practise the conversations.

(✱ 3.19)
G Oh, John! You didn't get the bread.
H No, I didn't, but I got some beer.

(✱ 3.20)
I What did you do last night?
J I went to the cinema.
I Who did you go with?
J Gary.
I What did you see?
J We saw *Star Wars Episode III*.

C Language focus

The past simple, irregular verbs

Positive

I	saw	it.
You	bought	them.
We	got	
They	went	there.
He		home.
She		to the shop.

Negative

I	didn't	see	it.
You		buy	them.
We		get	
They		go	there.
He			home.
She			to the shop.

Questions

Did	you	see	it?
	we	buy	them?
	they	get	
	he	go	there?
	she		home?
	I		to the shop?

Short answers

Yes, (I) did.
No, (we) didn't.

***Wh-* questions**

Where did (you) go?
Who did (she) see?
What did (they) buy?

1 Write negative answers.

What did you have? I didn't have anything.

1 What did you see?
2 What did you buy?
3 What did you get?
4 What did you do?

2 Write negative answers. You don't know the past tense of the verbs, but you can do the exercise!

1 What did you eat?
2 What did you drink?
3 What did you read?
4 What did you write?
5 What did you say?
6 What did you take?

D Talking about the past

1 **Ask and answer.**

- **The post**
  Did you get any post this morning?
  What did you get?
  Did you get ... ?
  - [ ] a bill   [ ] a business letter
  - [ ] a love letter   [ ] a postcard
  - [ ] a birthday card [ ] an advert

- **Shopping**
  When did you last go shopping?
  Where did you go?
  Which shops did you go to?
  Did you buy anything?
  What did you buy?

- **Films**
  When did you last see a film?   What was the film?
  Where did you see it?   Who did you go with?
  Who was in the film?   Was it good?

2 **What did you see on the way to this lesson?**
  Did you see ... ?
  - [ ] a dog   [ ] a police car   [ ] an ambulance   [ ] a bridge
  - [ ] a plane   [ ] your teacher   [ ] anything else?

See **Extension 29** p.180

30 Life events

A Photo album

1 Listen and read.
2 Underline all the past tense verbs.

✱ 3.21   I was born in London. My parents were too. My grandparents came to England from India about fifty years ago.

✱ 3.23   I went to school in Belfast. I finished school in 2002.

✱ 3.24   We moved to Manchester when I was twelve.

✱ 3.22   I started school when I was five.

✱ 3.25   We lived in Scotland for five years.

UNIT THIRTY

3 Complete the table. Which verbs are regular?

Present	Past	Present	Past
be born		learn	
come		move	
finish		pass	
get married		start	
live		study	
meet		work	

(✳ 3.26) I studied Geography at university.

(✳ 3.27) I learned to drive when I was eighteen. I didn't pass my test the first time, but I passed it the second time.

(✳ 3.28) My first job was in a shop. I worked there for two years.

(✳ 3.29) I met my girlfriend at a dance.

(✳ 3.30) We got married in Las Vegas.

B Language focus

The past simple, regular verbs
I pass**ed** my test.
He **didn't** pass his test.
Did you pass your test?

Spelling
Add -d or -ed to the present

add -ed	start → started work → worked
add -d	live → lived move → moved
change -y to -ied	study → studied
double letters	stop → stopped

Pronunciation
The final -d /-ed sounds like

/d/	live → lived
/t/	work → worked
/ɪd/	start → started

when
I started school when I was five.
I learned to drive when I was eighteen.

for
I lived there for three years.
I worked in a shop for two months.

Match the questions and the answers.

Question
1. When were you born?
2. When did you start school?
3. When did you get married?
4. How long did you live in Sydney?
5. Which university did you go to?
6. What did you study?

Answer
A Two weeks ago.
B Oxford.
C Mathematics.
D When I was five.
E In 1985.
F For five years.

C Pronunciation

Listen to the examples. (✱ 3.31)
/d/ lived, /t/ worked, /ɪd/ started

Listen. Write /t/, /d/ or /ɪd/ after the verbs. (✱ 3.31)

moved	....	worked	....	asked	....
finished	....	stopped	....	liked	....
learned	....	wanted	....	loved	....
started	....	passed	....	hated	....

D Happy birthday

1 Listen and complete the sentences. (✱ 3.32)

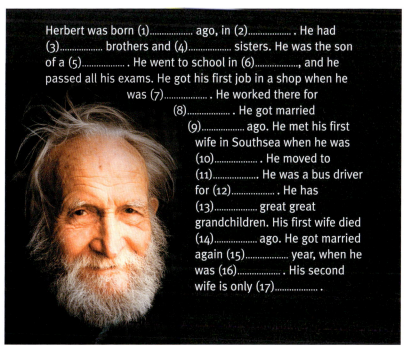

Herbert was born (1)............... ago, in (2)............... . He had (3)............... brothers and (4)............... sisters. He was the son of a (5)............... . He went to school in (6)..............., and he passed all his exams. He got his first job in a shop when he was (7)............... . He worked there for (8)............... . He got married (9)............... ago. He met his first wife in Southsea when he was (10)............... . He moved to (11)............... . He was a bus driver for (12)............... . He has (13)............... great great grandchildren. His first wife died (14)............... ago. He got married again (15)............... year, when he was (16)............... . His second wife is only (17)............... .

2 Ask and answer about Herbert.

When was he born?
Where was he born?
What was his father's job?
How many brothers did he have?
Where did he go to school?
When did he start work?
Where did he work?

Where did he meet his first wife?
When did he meet her?
When did they get married?
Where did he move to?
How long was he a bus driver?
When did his first wife die?
How old is his second wife?

E Writing

I was born in Russia. My family moved to Canada when I was very young. We lived in Toronto, and I started school there. When I was ten ...

1 Write about your life.

2 Pair work. Read about your partner's life. Ask questions for extra information.

3 Write about one of these people.
   - a relative
   - a friend
   - a famous person

See **Extension 30** p.181

**Extensions
Communication activities
Transcripts
Grammar**

in
English

EXTENSION 1

Hello

Complete the conversation.

Nick Hello. My ....'s Nick. What's .... name?
Kate ...., Nick. My name .... Kate.
Nick ....'s your phone number?
Kate My .... number's 0208 675 4401.

Reading

ANNA CARTER
PHOTOGRAPHER

Weddings • Portraits • Babies
Telephone: 01202 144879
Fax: 01202 144878
Mobile: 07973 586004

Adam Green
Astrologer to the stars
Offices in London,
L.A., Geneva
Telephone: 0207 140063
Fax: 0207 900864
Mobile: 07940 332176

Answer the questions.

1 What's her fax number?
2 What's his phone number?
3 What's her mobile number?

Sounds

Circle the word with the different vowel sound.

nine	my	(Nick)	five
/aɪ/	/aɪ/	/ɪ/	/aɪ/

/eɪ/	Kate	what	name	eight
/ɪ/	six	Nick	his	meet
/əʊ/	good	phone	don't	know
/aɪ/	Hi	nine	his	five

NAMES

Add (+) more English names.

Adam

Anna

EXTENSION 2

Jobs

Match the jobs and the pictures.

waiter   taxi driver   mechanic   police officer

Ask and answer about the pictures.
- What's her job?
- She's a police officer.

Say the words.

teacher waiter driver cleaner doctor student

alphabet

Say aloud.

R
O
Y I
U W Q
H A K J
X Z N M S L F
G V B T E G P D

Say the alphabet.
A B C D E F G H I J
K L M N O P Q R S T
U V W X Y Z

ABBREVIATIONS

Match the abbreviations.

British Broadcasting Corporation BBC
1 America On-Line ....
2 International Business Machines ....
3 European Union ....
4 Cable Network News ....
5 Donna Karan New York ....
6 Music Television ....

BBC   DKNY

MTV   CNN

EU   IBM

AOL   ....

Add more abbreviations.

Say the abbreviations aloud.

GRAMMAR

Underline the correct word.

1 What's (you / your / you're) name?
2 Are (you / your / you're) a doctor?
3 (You / Your / You're) a receptionist.
4 What's (he / his / he's) job?
5 (He / His / He's) a taxi driver.
6 (I / My / I'm) name's Lucy.
7 (I / My / I'm) a waiter.
8 (She / Her / She's) a police officer.
9 What's (she / her / she's) job?

EXTENSION 3

Quiz

Ask and answer.

1 Is Hong Kong in China?
2 Are you an office worker?
3 Is Toronto in the USA?
4 Is your teacher American?
5 Is Coca-Cola Canadian?
6 Is Sydney in Australia?
7 Is BMW German?
8 Can you translate 'Spain'?
9 Can you spell 'engineer'?
10 Is 'Disney' a first name?
11 Is 'Walt' a family name?
12 Are you a student?

COUNTRIES

Read and complete the table.

ENGLISH OR BRITISH?

English, Scottish and Welsh people are **British**. England, Scotland and Wales are in **Great Britain**.

England, Scotland, Wales and Northern Ireland are **The United Kingdom** (or UK). The Republic of **Ireland** isn't in the UK.

The UK and Ireland together are **The British Isles**.

Country	Nationality
Britain	British
England	
	Scottish
Wales	
	Irish

A party

Imagine. You're at a party. You're famous. Speak to students in your class.

▶ Hello, I'm (*Sarah Ferguson*). What's your name?
◀ Hello, (*Sarah*). I'm (*Steven Spielberg*). Where are you from?
▶ I'm from England. What's your job, (*Steven*)?
◀ I'm a (*film director*).

EXTENSION 4

Phrase books

Choose a phrase book for a learner of English.
Choose a phrase book for a tourist.
Choose ten phrases for you.

TEN ESSENTIAL PHRASES
1 Yes.
2 No.
3 Please.
4 Thank you.
5 I'm sorry.
6 What's (*this*) in English?
7 Do you speak (*French*)?
8 I don't speak English.
9 I don't understand.
10 Can you repeat that?

YOUR TOP TEN PHRASES
Yes. Please. Hello. No. Sorry. Goodbye Thanks. Excuse me. OK. I don't understand.

In a hotel

Complete the conversation.

You	Good evening.
Receptionist	Good evening, ………… .
You	Do you speak ………… ?
Receptionist	No, I'm sorry, I don't. What's your name, please?
You	………… .
Receptionist	Can you spell that?
You	………… .
Receptionist	Thank you. Where are you from?
You	………… in ………… .
Receptionist	This is your key. Have a nice evening.
You	………… . Goodnight.
Receptionist	Goodnight

Questions and answers

Match the questions and the answers.

Ask the questions. Say the answers.

Question
1 How are you?
2 Do you speak Italian?
3 Where are you from?
4 What's her name?
5 What's his job?

Answer
A He's an office worker.
B Mrs Ashton.
C I'm very well, thanks.
D Paris.
E No, sorry.

EXTENSION 5

INTERNATIONAL WORDS

Are these words the same or nearly the same in your language?

Put *a* or *an* with the words.

.... e-mail
.... bus
.... Apple computer
.... video
.... pizza

.... pub
.... television
.... airport
.... sandwich
.... taxi

.... restaurant
.... orchestra
.... Internet connection
.... hamburger
.... football

a / an

The sound of the next word is important.
an orange, **a S**panish orange
a computer, **an** Apple computer

Complete the sentences with *a* or *an*.

1 He's .... shop assistant.
2 She's .... office worker.
3 It's .... English video.
4 It's .... Italian passport.
5 It's .... Canadian orchestra.
6 It's .... IBM computer.
7 It's .... Agfa film.
8 It's .... Mexican orange.

Plurals: spelling

+ s	pens, oranges, umbrellas
+ es (after -ch /-ss/-z sound)	toothbrush → toothbrushes, class → classes
vowel → y + s	key → keys
consonant → y + ies	dictionary → dictionaries
fe → ves	penknife → penknives

Write the plurals.

camera	sandwich	day	watch	knife
....	....	....	....	....
office	envelope	city	nationality	taxi
....	....	....	....	....

EXTENSION 6

Conversations

Match a question and an answer with a picture.

Question
1 Tea or coffee?
2 Sorry, are you busy?
3 Where are we?
4 Anything else, madam?

Answer
A Yes. A sandwich, please.
B Sorry. I don't know.
C Yes. Just a minute.
D Coffee, please.

Practise the conversations.

GRAMMAR

Complete the sentences with *'m*, *'s* or *'re*.

1 It .... an English dictionary.
2 They .... Irish.
3 We .... in a hurry.
4 I .... a student.
5 She .... an office worker.
6 He .... from Scotland.
7 You .... busy.

Make negative sentences with *'m not*, *isn't* or *aren't*.

SOUNDS

Circle the word with the different vowel sound.

tea	(ten)	we	me
/iː/	/e/	/iː/	/iː/

/ɜː/	sir	her	first	we're
/e/	they	else	pen	menu
/eə/	they're	we're	where	airport
/ɪ/	minute	single	window	Chinese
/ʌ/	hurry	busy	just	umbrella

Stress

Underline the stress.

• • •   • • •
ham<u>bur</u>ger   com<u>pu</u>ter

envelope
umbrella
journalist
assistant
restaurant

INTERNATIONAL FOOD

Underline the languages and circle the countries.

Pizza is on menus in Italy, England, Mexico, and Japan. Is *pizza* an Italian word? Yes, it is. But now it's also English, Spanish, and Japanese. The words *pasta* and *spaghetti* are also from Italian. *Sandwich* is from English, *whisky* is from the Scottish language, Gaelic, and *hamburger* is from American English. It isn't from German. *Yoghurt* is from Turkish. *Vodka* is from Russian. *Chocolate* is from Nahuatl, a native American language from Mexico. You can have sushi in restaurants in Britain, the USA, and France. The word *sushi* is from Japanese.

Vocabulary tip

Are these words the same or nearly the same in your language?

burger	hot dog	tea
coffee	salad	cola
fries	yoghurt	pasta
sandwich	whisky	vodka
donut	chocolate	pizza
spaghetti	espresso	sushi
croissant	cappucino	
cheeseburger		

Remember words in groups. Complete the diagram.

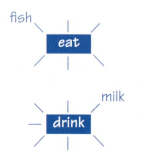

Coffee shop

Role play a conversation.

COFFEE SHOP

Filter coffee	$2.00
Espresso	$1.80
Double Espresso	$3.00
Capuccino	$2.40
English breakfast tea	$2.10
Chocolate muffin	$2.90
Chocolate chip cookie	$1.80
Croissant	$2.40
Donut	$1.20

Colours

Underline the colours.

Classic rock songs
'Long Black Limousine' – Elvis Presley
'Green Green Grass of Home' – Tom Jones
'Pink Cadillac' – Bruce Springsteen
'Black & White' – Michael Jackson
'Brown Sugar' – The Rolling Stones
'Yellow River' – Tony Christie
'Blue Moon' – The Marcels
'Red Red Wine' – UB40
'Little Red Corvette' – Prince
'Old Brown Shoe' – The Beatles
'Yellow' – Coldplay
'Grey Day' – Madness

GRAMMAR

Make sentences.

car / It / a / 's / big
It's a big car.

1 Are / shoes? / they / new
2 printer. / It / colour / a / is
3 jeans. / 're / blue / They
4 film. / white / It / black / and / is / a
5 man. / He / an / angry / is
6 card. / It / yellow / 's / a
7 cold. / 'm / I
8 tap? / a / cold / Is / it

a / an

Complete the sentences with *a* or *an*.

1 It's .... American car.
2 He's .... old man.
3 It's .... small airport.
4 It's .... black and white film.
5 She's .... unhappy customer.
6 It's .... red apple.
7 It's .... orange shirt.

and / & / 'n'

Write ▸ black and white or
        black & white
Say   black 'n' /n/ white

Say these with /n/.

black & white   rock & roll
fish & chips   milk & sugar
red & yellow   blue & green
pink & white

Vocabulary tip

Remember opposites. *new – old*.
Match the opposites.

hot   big
white   cold
small   black

In your vocabulary notebook, write words with the opposites.

yes   no
stop   go
high   low

EXTENSION 9

Hotel information

Read the information.

Answer the questions.

1 Is there a mini-bar in room 1990?
2 Is there a bath in room 1660?
3 Are there four rooms in room 1330?
4 Is room 1555 a single room?
5 Are there any phones in room 1440?
6 Where's the sauna?

Describe Room 1880.

PREPOSITIONS

in   on   by

Make questions.

books / on / table
Are there any books on the table?

armchair / in / room
Is there an armchair in the room?

1 picture / on / wall
2 lights / by / bed
3 towels / in / bathroom
4 shirts / in / wardrobe
5 restaurant / in / hotel
6 carpet / on / floor

Vocabulary tip

Write words in lists.
Put these words in the lists.

taps   wardrobe   shower   bed
carpet   toilet   toothbrushes

In the bedroom   **In the bathroom**

....
....
....
....

Add more words to the lists.

EXTENSION 10

PRICES

Guess prices for your country.
Ask about your partner's survey.

- ▶ How much are jeans?
- ◀ They're about … .
- ▶ How much is a Big Mac?
- ◀ It's about … .

SHOPPING SURVEY

Do you know prices?

- a CD (in the Top 20)
- a Big Mac (burger)
- jeans (Levi's)
- trainers (Nike)
- an English dictionary (Oxford)
- a litre of petrol (gasoline)
- a Mars bar (chocolate)

GRAMMAR

Underline the correct word.

1 What's (his / he's / him) name?
2 This postcard is for (she / her / she's).
3 (I'm / My / Me) from Italy.
4 The hot dog's for (I / my / me).
5 Thank (you / your / you're) for the coffee.
6 The shoes aren't for (he / his / him). They're for her.
7 It's the phone. It's for (you / your / you're).
8 He's (me / I / my) friend.
9 Excuse (I / my / me). I'm very sorry.

Singular and plural

In English, *jeans* are plural, *shirt* is singular.

Underline the plural words.

jeans	dress
shoes	trousers
top	boots
shorts	shirt
trainers	jacket
skirt	T-shirt

Read the text

Write the text with *she*.
She's a student at …

'I'm a student at Manchester University. This is my room. There's a single bed, a desk, a chair, and a wardrobe. There's a brown carpet on the floor. I've got a computer. It's on my desk. There's a photograph of my family on the wall near my bed. I've got some books and some CDs. They're on the floor. I haven't got a telephone and I haven't got a TV.'

Sounds

Have you got an EU passport?
Have you got an MP3 player?
Have you got a US passport?
She's got an S-type Jaguar.

***an* before the *sound* of vowels**
EU – /iː juː/   MP – /em piː/
ID – /aɪ diː/   S-type – /es taɪp/

***a* before the *sound* of consonants**
US – /juː es/   UN – /juː en/

Complete the sentences with *a* or *an*.
1 Look! There's .... UFO!
2 He's got .... *X-Files* video.
3 She's got .... MG sports car.
4 They've got .... e-mail address.
5 It's .... F 111 airplane.

GRAMMAR

Underline the correct word.
1 (Have / Has) she got a picture?
2 Have you got (any / some / a) keys?
3 He hasn't (not / got) any books.
4 (Have / Has) they got the right tickets?
5 There (are / have) some pens on the table.
6 (Has / Is) there a phone?
7 He hasn't got (a / some / any) driving licence.

THE ROYLE FAMILY

Read and write the names.

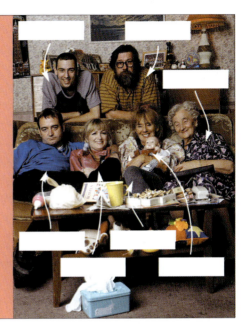

The Royle Family is a popular British TV programme. Jim Royle is married to Barbara. They've got two children. Their daughter's name is Denise, and she's married to Dave. They've got a baby boy. Anthony is Denise's brother. He's seventeen. Norma is Denise's grandmother. She's Barbara's mother. They're from Manchester.

Answer the questions.
1 Who is Jim's son?
2 What's Denise's husband's name?
3 Who is Norma?
4 Who is Anthony's sister?
5 How old is Anthony?
6 Where are they from?

FAMILY

Complete the sentences.
1 Your mother's brother is your ....
2 Your father's sister is your ....
3 Your brother's daughter is your ....
4 Your sister's son is your ....
5 Your uncle's son is your ....
6 Your aunt's daughter is your ....
7 Your father's mother is your ....
8 Your mother's father is your ....

Stress

Say aloud.

● ●
parent

● ● ●
grandparent

● ●
father

● ● ●
grandfather

mother
grandmother
daughter
granddaughter
son
grandson
children
grandchildren

Learning English

Look at the tips. Put:
(✔) Yes, I agree.
(✗) No, I don't agree.
(?) I don't know.

TIPS FOR LEARNING ENGLISH
- Listen to CDs or cassettes.
- Repeat words and sentences from CDs or cassettes.
- Practise audio exercises on CD.
- Don't translate every word.
- Use a monolingual (English-English) dictionary.
- Use a translation dictionary (English-your language).
- Write new words in a vocabulary notebook.
- Translate new words and sentences.
- Watch videos, films, and TV programmes in English.
- Read English books, magazines, and newspapers.
- Use the Internet. Look at websites in English.
- Listen to songs in English.

Have you got any more tips?

Opposites

Match the opposites.

sit down — stand up
stop — go
open — close
go out — come in
turn on — turn off

turn on / turn off

Add words to the diagram.
Compare with a partner.

turn on — the tap
turn off

GRAMMAR

Tick (✔) the correct word.

1 This is a photo of (☐ we ☐ us).
2 (☐ We ☐ Us) are in Disney World in Orlando.
3 Are (☐ their ☐ them) books on the table?
4 Look at (☐ she ☐ her). Is she a rock star?
5 (☐ They ☐ Them) 're from England.
6 Excuse (☐ I ☐ me), do you speak French?
7 Is (☐ he ☐ him) from Spain?
8 (☐ Our ☐ Us) family is from Ireland.
9 This is Mr and Mrs Smith. Do you know (☐ they ☐ them)?
10 This is a photo of our children. Look at (☐ they ☐ them).

Football star

Read the text.

Tick (✔) the true sentences. Correct the false sentences.

- ☐ He plays for France.
- ☐ He lives in Manchester.
- ☐ He doesn't live in Paris.
- ☐ He lives in a small flat.
- ☐ He lives alone.
- ☐ He lives in Blackpool.
- ☐ He doesn't play for Manchester United.

Make ten sentences about sports people and rock stars.

(*He*) plays for (*name of football club*).
(*She*) plays in (*name of rock group*).

Marc Perrier

This is Marc Perrier. Marc is French, and he is a French international footballer. He plays for Manchester United. He doesn't live in Manchester. He lives in a big house in Blackpool with his family. He's got two daughters. He's got a flat in Paris, but he doesn't live there.

GRAMMAR

Tick (✔) the correct word.

1 They (☐ live ☐ lives) in Hong Kong.
2 They (☐ don't ☐ doesn't) work in Hong Kong.
3 She (☐ work ☐ works) in a bank.
4 He doesn't (☐ work ☐ works) in a bank.
5 Does he (☐ work ☐ works) in a hotel?
6 Yes, he (☐ does ☐ do).

Sounds

Circle the word with the different vowel sound.

goes	(does)	don't	know
/əʊ/	/ʌ/	/əʊ/	/əʊ/

/uː/	do	you	go	to
/ʌ/	us	does	up	down
/ɒ/	hospital	hotel	college	off
/eə/	say	parents	careful	their
/ɜː/	work	forget	turn	word

Writing

Add apostrophes (').

1 He hasnt got a brother.
2 We dont live near them.
3 Ive got two uncles.
4 My aunts name is Anna.
5 She doesnt know him.
6 I havent got any cousins.
7 Theyre from Ireland.
8 Wheres the bathroom?
9 Whats your name?

EXTENSION 15

Opening and closing times

SAN FRANCISCO TOURIST INFORMATION

Visitor Information Center
Hallidie Plaza, Powell St & Market St
9 a.m. to 5.30 p.m. on weekdays
9 a.m. to 3 p.m. on Saturdays
10 a.m. to 2 p.m. on Sundays

Banks
Banks are open from 10 a.m. to 3 p.m. Monday to Friday. They do not close for lunch.

Some banks open at 7.30 a.m., and some close at 6 p.m. Some banks are open on Saturday mornings.

Post offices
The General Mail Facility at 1300 Evans Avenue opens at 8 a.m. Monday to Friday, and closes at 6 p.m. Opening hours are from 8 a.m. to 5 p.m. on Saturday.

Businesses
Businesses are open from 9 a.m. to 5 p.m. on weekdays. They do not close for lunch.

Stores
Stores are open from 10 a.m. to 6 p.m. Monday to Saturday. Some malls and large stores are open in the evening and on Sundays. Stores are very busy from 12 to 2 p.m., and on Saturdays.

Read the information.

Spelling note:
centre (UK) / center (USA)

Complete these sentences with *at, on, from, to.*

In San Francisco …
1. Post offices are closed ………… Sundays.
2. Stores are very busy ………… 12 to 2 p.m.
3. Some banks open ………… 7.30 a.m.
4. Some banks close ………… 6 p.m.
5. Businesses are open from 9 a.m. to 5 p.m. ………… weekdays.
6. The Visitor Information Center is open from 10 a.m. ………… 2 p.m. on Sundays.

Find this information.

1. What are the opening hours of the post office on weekdays?
2. What time does the Visitor Information Center close on Saturdays?
3. What time do stores open on weekdays?

Writing

Write about your town.

In my town, stores are open from 10 a.m. to 6 p.m. Monday to Saturday. They don't open on Sundays. Offices open at 9 a.m. and close at 5 p.m. They don't close for lunch. Banks and post offices are closed on Sundays.

EXTENSION 16

VOCABULARY

Match the words from column A and column B.

A	B
traffic	park
taxi	station
car	box
railway	rank
telephone	mall
driving	lights
shopping	licence

Days and numbers

Complete the sentences.

Monday is the first day of the week.
Tuesday is the .... day of the week.
.... is the third day of the week.
Thursday is the .... day of the week.
Friday is the .... day of the week.
.... is the sixth day of the week.
Sunday is the .... day of the week.

Sounds

Circle the word with the different consonant sound.

	thank /θ/	third /θ/	(the) /ð/	eighth /θ/
/ð/	there	thirty	that	them
/θ/	this	fifth	three	Thursday
/dʒ/	German	Japan	girl	juice
/tʃ/	shop	chocolate	church	chair
/ʃ/	she	shop	shorts	cheese

Questions and answers

Match the questions and the answers.

Question	Answer
1 How much is the dress?	A Nine thirty.
2 What time does it open?	B In a hospital.
3 Where's their flat?	C Two.
4 Where does she work?	D I have.
5 What colour are his shorts?	E It's on the fifth floor.
6 How many sisters has she got?	F Light blue.
7 Who's got a car?	G Twenty-five fifty.

OPPOSITES

High is the opposite of *low*.

Find the opposite of these words in the word square.

up   black   cold   left   big
new   open   on   in

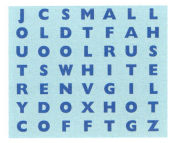

EXTENSION 17

On Sunday

Talk about your Sunday.
I have breakfast in bed. I get up late.

get up late

read the newspapers

wash the car

THINGS TO DO ... ON SUNDAY

have a big lunch

watch an old film

have a sleep

SOUNDS

Put the words in the correct columns.

finishes	starts	watches
goes	lives	works
plays	opens	closes
gives	does	gets up
has	reads	washes

/s/	/z/	/ɪz/
starts	lives	closes

* the /ɪz/ sound comes after the sounds s /s/, sh /ʃ/, j /dʒ/ and ch /tʃ/.

Education in Britain

Read about British schools.

British children start school at five years old. They go to school in the mornings and afternoons. School starts at 9 a.m. and finishes at 3.30 p.m. They have one hour for lunch, and they have a morning break and an afternoon break. They don't go to school on Saturdays. They go to secondary school at twelve (or eleven in some towns). They have important exams at sixteen and eighteen. Some students finish school at sixteen, and some students finish at eighteen. Students go to university at eighteen.

Write about schools in your country.

EXTENSION 18

Questions and answers

Match the questions and the answers. Ask the questions. Say the answers.

Question
1 Can I have the pepper?
2 I'd like some wine, please.
3 Have you got a vegetarian meal?
4 Would you like this table or that one?
5 Would you like sugar in your tea?
6 Who is it for?
7 How much is it?
8 What would you like to drink?
9 Which dessert would you like?

Answer
A Yes, there's pasta with tomato sauce.
B No, thank you.
C Yes, here you are.
D Nine fifty.
E A glass of champagne, please.
F The chocolate cake, please.
G That one. By the window.
H Red or white?
I It's for me.

Menu

Write a menu. Choose:
three drinks   three starters
three main courses three desserts

Use your menu and make a conversation.
Waiter Which starter would you like?
You ....
Waiter Which main course would you like?
You ....
Waiter We haven't got that. I'm sorry.
You Have .... ?
Waiter Yes, we have. Would you like that?
You ....
Waiter Would you like some wine with your meal?
You ....
Waiter That's fine.

Question words

Put the question words in the sentences.

Who   Where   What   How much   Which   When

1 .... that? That's Jane. She's my sister.
2 .... is that? It's a calculator.
3 .... is it? It's five twenty-five.
4 .... do they start work? At 8.30.
5 .... book would you like?
   This one or that one?
6 .... do they live? They live in Manchester.

VOCABULARY

Match the words.

A	D
green	wine
black	cake
mineral	cola
chocolate	juice
orange	salad
milk	water
red	shake
diet	pepper

EXTENSION 19

Chimps can communicate

CHIMPANZEES are very intelligent, but they can't speak because they can't make the right sounds. They can communicate with sign language. Panbanisha, a female chimp in Atlanta, can use a computer. The computer has got 400 coloured keys. Some keys have pictures like 'apple' and some keys have symbols for words like 'give me', 'want', 'good', 'where', 'my', and 'help'.

Panbanisha can understand spoken English, and she can answer on the computer. She knows 3,000 words, and she can make sentences like, 'Can I have an iced coffee?' Panbanisha can write some of the symbols. Panbanisha's son, Nyota, can use the computer too. His mother is his teacher.

Answer the questions.
1 Why can't chimps speak?
2 How can chimps communicate?
3 Where does Panbanisha live?
4 What can she do?
5 Can she understand spoken English?
6 How can she answer?
7 How many words does she know?
8 Do you know 3,000 words in English?
9 What's her son's name?
10 Can he use the computer?

ANSWERPHONE

Complete the sentences with *can* or *can't*.

Hello. We .... answer your call at the moment. We're busy. You .... leave a message after the tone. You .... fax us on 01202 100698, or you .... e-mail us on jsmith@supernet.co.uk.

Write an answerphone message for your phone. Say it aloud.

EXTENSION 20

time

How many words can you add to the word map? Stop after three minutes.

at / on / in

Complete the sentences with *at*, *on*, or *in*.

1 Children don't go to school .... August.
2 Can I see the doctor .... the afternoon?
3 That bank is closed .... Saturdays.
4 I have a bath .... the evening.
5 She goes to bed .... eleven o'clock.
6 She lives .... Barcelona.
7 They're .... their honeymoon.

Months

Answer about you / your country.

1 Which month is your birthday?
2 Which month do schools start?
3 Which month do schools finish?
4 Which month has got 28 or 29 days?
5 Which are the hot months?
6 Which are the cold months?

SOUNDS

Can you say these aloud?

1 Thursday the thirtieth at three thirty.
2 Friday the fifteenth of February at four fifty.
3 Saturday the seventh of September at sixteen seventeen.
4 The thirty-first is a Thursday.

EXTENSION 21

Automatic postcard

Complete the postcard.

New words

In English, we can make verbs from 'new' words. For example, words like *video*, *fax*, *e-mail*. Can you do this in your language? *We can say ...*

I'm videoing a programme.
Can you fax me tomorrow morning?
She's faxing me the information.
Who are you e-mailing?
The computer's digitizing the photo.
Please scan this picture for me.

SPELLING

Put the verbs in the correct groups.

close   drive   go   have   live   open   put   shop   sing   swim   work

+ ing	-e, + ing	double the letter (e.g. t → *tt*) + ing
eat / eating	phone / phoning	sit / sitting

Because ...

Can you make seven sentences from this table?

He	can't	answer the phone	because	he	is taking off.
She		see you today		she	doesn't speak English.
		work in the library		the plane	is closed today.
		use a mobile phone		it	hasn't got a licence.
		understand			is having a bath.
		e-mail me			hasn't got a computer.
		drive			is busy.

EXCUSES

Write their excuses.
A No, I'm afraid I can't. It's my brother's birthday. I'm having lunch with him.
B Sorry, I've got plans. ....
C I'm sorry, I'm not free on Saturday. ....
D No, sorry, I can't. ....
E Sorry, I'm busy on Saturday. ....

Sounds

Circle the word with the different vowel sound.

near	here	(hair)	we're
/ɪə/	/ɪə/	/eə/	/ɪə/

/e/	friend	seat	when	next
/æ/	plan	have	play	salad
/ɑː/	father	bar	car	late
/aʊ/	your	now	shower	hour
/ɔː/	course	house	August	awful

FUTURE TIME WORDS

Complete the table in the correct order.

next year
tomorrow evening
next month
tomorrow afternoon
next week
tomorrow morning

	now
F	tonight
U	
T	
U	
R	
E	

EXTENSION 23

Entertainment guide

Twelfth Night
by William Shakespeare
National Theatre
23rd July – 31st August

TWENTIETH CENTURY ART EXHIBITION
Museum of Modern Art
15th June – 22nd June

Beethoven's FIFTH SYMPHONY
Queen Elizabeth Hall
September 30th

ENGLAND v POLAND
The Millennium Stadium
11th July 3 o'clock

Classic film: Orson Welles in
THE THIRD MAN
Empire Cinema
8th July – 15th July

Mozart
THE MAGIC FLUTE
Royal Opera House
9th July – 30th July

Find this information.
1 What's the title of the Shakespeare play?
2 What time does the football match start?
3 Where can you see *The Third Man*?
4 Which symphony is on at the Queen Elizabeth Hall?
5 When does the art exhibition finish?
6 What's the date of the classical concert?
7 Which Beethoven symphony are they playing?
8 What is *The Magic Flute*?
9 Can you see the film on 16th July?

for / *to*

Put the words in the correct columns. Can you add more?

a coffee   a pub   McDonald's
a drink   a restaurant   a beer
The Hard Rock Café   a swim
the shopping mall

Let's go for …	Let's go to …
a pizza	the cinema

Do you like …? / *Would you like …?*

Do you like …? is a *question*.
Would you like …? is an *offer*.

▶ Do you like tea?
◀ Yes, I do.
▶ Would you like some tea now?
◀ No, thanks. Not at the moment.

Make conversations with these words.

coffee   wine   popcorn

DO YOU LIKE TRAVELLING?

Here are some opinions. Who says them? Write A, B, or C.

A Martin is a sales executive. He's 44.
B Laura is a flight attendant. She's 31.
C Bob is a student. He's 20.

There isn't a 'correct' answer. It's your opinion.

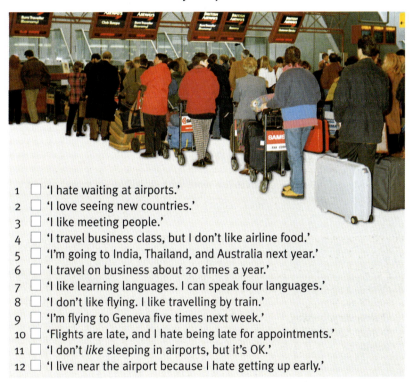

1. ☐ 'I hate waiting at airports.'
2. ☐ 'I love seeing new countries.'
3. ☐ 'I like meeting people.'
4. ☐ 'I travel business class, but I don't like airline food.'
5. ☐ 'I'm going to India, Thailand, and Australia next year.'
6. ☐ 'I travel on business about 20 times a year.'
7. ☐ 'I like learning languages. I can speak four languages.'
8. ☐ 'I don't like flying. I like travelling by train.'
9. ☐ 'I'm flying to Geneva five times next week.'
10. ☐ 'Flights are late, and I hate being late for appointments.'
11. ☐ 'I don't *like* sleeping in airports, but it's OK.'
12. ☐ 'I live near the airport because I hate getting up early.'

Questions and answers

Match the questions and the answers. Ask the questions. Say the answers.

Question
1. What are you doing tomorrow?
2. How about going to the cinema?
3. Do you like swimming?
4. Where are you going?
5. When does the film finish?
6. What's the date tomorrow?

Answer
A Yes, I love them.
B To a friend's house.
C At ten thirty, I think.
D I'm staying in. Why?
E It's the thirty-first.
F Great. What's on?

EXTENSION 25

NEXT WEEKEND

Interview a partner. Complete the questionnaire.

1 What are you going to do on Saturday morning?
- ❏ work
- ❏ get up late
- ❏ meet friends
- ❏ go shopping
- ❏ other _____

2 What are you going to do on Saturday evening?
- ❏ watch TV
- ❏ go to a bar or restaurant
- ❏ go to a club
- ❏ have dinner with friends
- ❏ go to the cinema
- ❏ wash my hair
- ❏ stay in
- ❏ other _____

3 Where are you going to have lunch on Sunday?
- ❏ at home
- ❏ at work
- ❏ in a restaurant
- ❏ with friends
- ❏ with my family
- ❏ other _____

gonna / going to

going to sounds like *gonna*.
In rock songs, they write *gonna*.
Don't do this, but understand it and say it.

| Write | going to |
| Say | going to /gəʊɪŋ tə/ or gonna /gənə/ |

Say the song titles aloud.

'Everything's Gonna Be Alright' (Sweetbox, UK)
'I'm Gonna Make You a Star' (David Essex, UK)
'I'm Gonna Make You Love Me' (Diana Ross, USA)
'It's Gonna Take Some Time' (Carole King, USA)

Say the titles again with *going to*.

Sounds

Circle the word with the different vowel sound.

| look | **cup** | would | woman |
| /ʊ/ | /ʌ/ | /ʊ/ | /ʊ/ |

/ʌ/	month	some	Sunday	busy
/uː/	club	June	July	flu
/ʊ/	football	bus	book	good
/ɔɪ/	fall	boy	point	toilet
/ɔː/	popcorn	August	church	four

do / to do / doing

Tick (✓) the correct word.

1 I (❏ like ❏ to like ❏ liking) swimming.
2 It's (❏ go ❏ to go ❏ going) to rain.
3 I can (❏ speak ❏ to speak ❏ speaking) English.
4 I don't (❏ know ❏ to know ❏ knowing) them.
5 It's going (❏ be ❏ to be ❏ being) hot tomorrow.
6 I'd (❏ like ❏ to like ❏ liking) a drink.

EXTENSION 26

QUIZ

Do the quiz with a partner.

FILM
Who was the director of *Star Wars*?
A Steven Spielberg
B Harrison Ford
C George Lucas

SPORT
Who were the World Cup winners in 2002?
A France
B Germany
C Brazil

HISTORY
Who was the Queen of England in 1900?
A Queen Elizabeth
B Queen Victoria
C Queen Mary

POPULAR CULTURE
Who was Mickey Mouse's girlfriend?
A Daisy
B Cinderella
C Minnie

MUSIC
What were The Beatles' names?
A Noel, Vera, Chuck, Dave
B John, Paul, Mick, Keith
C John, Paul, George, Ringo

NATURAL WORLD
What were *Stegosaurus*, *Tyrannosaurus* and *Diplodocus*?
A birds
B dinosaurs
C mammals

SCIENCE AND TECHNOLOGY
Where was Einstein from?
A Switzerland
B Hungary
C Germany

Time words

Complete the table.

Present	Past
tonight	last night
this month	
this Sunday	
today	
this weekend	

SOUNDS

The unstressed sound /ə/ in /wəz/ and /wə/ is very common in English.

Say these words aloud.

Stressed sound	**Unstressed sound**
was /wɒz/	was /wəz/
were /wɜː/	were /wə/
have /hæv/	have /həv/
has /hæz/	has /həz/
can /kæn/	can /kən/
from /frɒm/	from /frəm/

Are the words stressed (S) or unstressed (U) in these sentences?

1 Have /həv/ you got any matches?
2 Yes, I have /hæv/.
3 He was /wəz/ tired.
4 Was /wəz/ she there? Yes, she was /wɒz/.
5 They were /wə/ in London yesterday.
6 Yes, we were /wɜː/ !
7 Can /kən/ you swim?
8 Yes, I can /kæn/.
9 Has /həz/ she got a boyfriend?
10 Where are they from /frɒm/?
11 She's from /frəm/ Mexico.

Postcard

INSTANT POSTCARD JUST TICK THE CORRECT BOXES.

Hi _____ ! We're here in _____ !
The journey was … ❏ very good ❏ OK ❏ awful.
The plane was … ❏ new ❏ very big ❏ very old.
The food on the plane was …
❏ very good ❏ not bad ❏ cold.
The films on the plane were …
❏ fantastic ❏ awful ❏ black and white.
The other passengers were … ❏ business people
❏ families with small children ❏ football fans.
The flight was …
❏ on time ❏ 30 minutes late ❏ 12 hours late.
Wish … ❏ you were ❏ we weren't here.

QUESTION AND ANSWER

Match the questions and the answers. Ask the questions. Say the answers.

Question

1 How long was your flight?
2 How many films were there on the flight?
3 Where were you last night?
4 Who was with you?
5 When were they in London?
6 What was the weather like?

Answer

A At the cinema.
B Last summer.
C Three.
D About ten hours.
E Very cold.
F My sister.

Vocabulary

Circle the different word.

weather	cloudy	windy	cold
hotel	beach	villa	apartment
January	August	May	month
flight	plane	train	car
café	food	buffet	restaurant
June	autumn	spring	winter

SOUNDS

The unstressed sound /ə/ in /wəz/ and /wə/ is in many English words.

Say these words aloud.

American   England   doctor
water   hospital   tomorrow
banana   cinema   summer

Underline the /ə/ sounds.

Scotland   teacher   lottery
newspaper   yesterday winter
alone   daughter   afternoon

EXTENSION 28

The year 1000

In the year 1000, life in England was very different. What things did they have? What didn't they have? Which of these things are true?
(The answers are at the end of the transcripts.)

- They didn't have sugar, pepper, tea, coffee, chocolate, tomatoes, or potatoes.
- They had beer with their meals, because water was dirty.
- They had English grapes and English wine.
- They didn't have plates. They put pieces of dry bread on the table, and put the food on the bread.
- They didn't have left and right shoes. All shoes were the same.
- They had bright yellow, green, red and brown clothes, but they didn't have many blue clothes. Blue clothes were very expensive. In paintings, rich and important people are wearing blue.
- They had money. In the year 1000 there was more silver money in England than in any country in Europe.
- They didn't have the number 'zero'.
- They had games of chess.

Make sentences about your country in the year 1000. Use *had / didn't have*.

Writing

Choose.
1. a woman's first name (e.g. *Sarah*)
2. a country
3. a time
4. a drink
5. a flavour of ice-cream
6. a day of the week
7. a colour
8. a meal
9. a man's first name
10. an age (e.g. *21*)

COMMUNICATION ACTIVITIES

Look at Activity 21 on p.202. Complete the story with your words.

Read your story to a partner.

EXTENSION 29

Oh, dear!

Josh was a politics student at Georgetown University in Washington D.C. Last summer he got a job in the White House. On the first Monday a new machine arrived in Josh's office. It was a document shredder, a machine that cuts up documents into small pieces. On Tuesday morning, Josh went to work early. He went into the office and saw the President! The President was next to the new machine. He had some documents in his hand.

'I don't understand this machine,' said the President, 'Why did they buy it?'

'It's easy, sir,' said Josh, 'Put the paper in here.'

The President did.

'Now, sir, push this green button.'

The President did. The machine started.

'Great,' he said, 'This is my new speech to The United Nations. I wrote it last night. By hand. It took me five hours. It's very important. I want ten photocopies, please.'

Find the past tenses of these verbs.

| say | arrive | do | write | take | start |

Can you tell the story with different names?
1 Change 'President' to your boss or head teacher.
2 Change 'Josh' to a female name.
3 This time, the person thinks it's a fax machine.

SOUNDS

Circle the word with the different vowel sound.

	saw	bought	(socks)	organic
	/ɔː/	/ɔː/	/ɒ/	/ɔː/
/e/	went	sell	want	bread
/aɪ/	villa	buy	why	flight
/əʊ/	post	frozen	got	toast
/ɑː/	party	father	train	last
/ɜː/	early	haircut	birthday	sir
/ʌ/	sugar	pub	buffet	under

Vocabulary tip

Learn the past tense of new verbs. Make a vocabulary notebook for lessons 28 and 29.

Vocabulary notebook
VERBS

Present	Past
am / is	was
are	
has / have	
go / goes	
do / does	
buy	
get	
see	

EXTENSION 30

A Mother Teresa

B Arnold Schwarzenegger

C Bill Gates

D Princess Diana

Twentieth century faces

Look at the photographs. Write A, B, C, or D.
1. ☐ Born in Austria in 1947.
2. ☐ Born in Seattle in 1955.
3. ☐ Born in England in 1961.
4. ☐ Born in Albania in 1910.
5. ☐ Lived in India.
6. ☐ Died in Calcutta in 1997.
7. ☐ Died in Paris in 1997.
8. ☐ Started Microsoft in 1975.
9. ☐ Moved to the United States.
10. ☐ Starred in action films.
11. ☐ Helped many poor people.
12. ☐ Got married to a prince in 1981.
13. ☐ Went to Harvard University for only one year.
14. ☐ Opened 'Planet Hollywood' restaurants.
15. ☐ Had two sons, William and Harry.
16. ☐ Was Mr Universe when he was 20.
17. ☐ Started programming computers when he was 13.

(The answers are at the end of the transcripts.)

GRAMMAR

**Complete the sentences.
Use the words from the box.**

for   about   when   in   ago

1. They started school .... they were five.
2. She lived in Brazil .... five years.
3. I learned to drive three years ....
4. They got married in Honolulu .... 1999.
5. She moved here six years ....

SOUNDS

Circle the word with the different final sound.

(wanted)   moved   loved   played
/ɪd/   /d/   /d/   /d/

/ɪd/	wanted	finished	started	hated
/t/	worked	stopped	liked	lived
/ɪz/	watches	opens	closes	washes
/d/	asked	loved	finished	opened

ACTIVITY ONE

Unit two. Student A

Ask student B.
Can you spell (hello)?

Say *You're right* **or** *You're wrong.*

ACTIVITY TWO

183

Unit five. Student A

With Student B look at your pictures for ten seconds.
Then answer Student B's questions.

Student A   Picture one.
Student B   Are they (watches)?
Student A   Yes, they are. / No, they aren't.

With Student B look at Student B's pictures for ten seconds.
Close your book. Ask student B questions.

Student B   Picture one.
Student A   Are they (umbrellas)?
Student B   Yes, they are. / No, they aren't.

ACTIVITY THREE

Unit nine. Student A

This is your room. Describe your room to Student B.

Find the different things.
Ask Student B questions about his / her picture.

Is there (an armchair)?
Are there any (apples)?
What colour is (the telephone)?
What colour are (the walls)?

ACTIVITY FOUR

Unit ten. Student A

Ask about Student B's pictures. Make notes.

jeans	size	colour	how much
shirt	size	colour	how much
trainers	size	colour	how much
sweatshirt	size	colour	how much

XS – £43.99

S – £59.25

L – £311

34 – £5.99

Answer Student B's questions.

ACTIVITY FIVE

Unit sixteen. Student A

You are at the station. Give Student B directions to these places.
the central car park
the church
the supermarket
Burger Land

Ask Student B for directions to these places.
the hospital
the bank
the post office
the ABC cinema

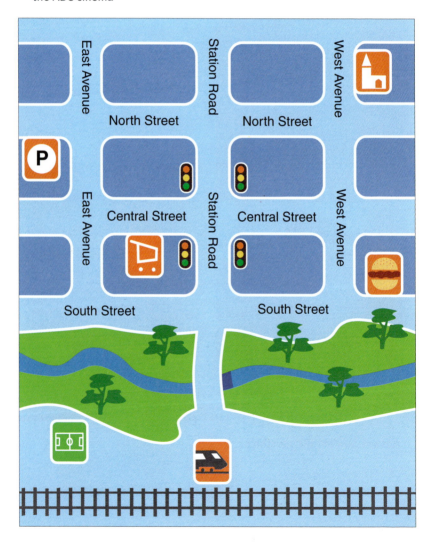

ACTIVITY SIX

Unit twenty. Student A

Look at the diary. You are Ms Cooper's secretary.
Student B wants an appointment.

Student B has a diary from Monday 11th to Sunday 17th February.
Ask Student B questions and make an appointment with Mr Freeman.

MONDAY 21 AUGUST
morning	In Rome
lunch	European conference
afternoon	
evening	Return Flight BA 557, 18.30

TUESDAY 22 AUGUST
morning	8.30 – 10.30 Mr Dickens
	10.45 – 12.30 Marketing meeting
lunch	Mrs Murdoch 12.45
afternoon	2.00 Miss Austen
	2.30 – 5.00 Bank manager
evening	finish 5.15

WEDNESDAY 23 AUGUST
morning	8.30 – 11.00 Ms Eliot
	11.00 – 1.00 FREE
lunch	Mr Lawrence 1.00 – 2.00
afternoon	2.15 Sales meeting (to 5.30 or 6.00)
evening	Finish 6.00

THURSDAY 24 AUGUST
morning	meeting Birmingham office
lunch	all day
afternoon	
evening	Return on 19.30 train

FRIDAY 25 AUGUST
morning	start 10.00
	10.15 – 12.00 Mrs Wilde
	12.00 – 12.45 Free
lunch	1.00 – 2.00 Mr Keats
afternoon	2.15 – 2.45 Free
	2.45 – 3.15 Mr Shelley
evening	3.15 – 4.30 Mr Byron
	Finish 5.30

SATURDAY 26 AUGUST
Not at work

SUNDAY 27 AUGUST
Not at work

ACTIVITY SEVEN

Unit twenty-one. Student A

Find these in your picture:

the young man   the businessman
the boy   the old man and the old woman
the girl   the dog
the young woman

Answer Student B's questions about your picture.

Student B's picture has got the same people. Ask about them.

What is the young man doing?

ACTIVITY EIGHT

Unit twenty-four. Student A

Read the answer to a puzzle. Don't tell the class!

Miss Anna Green likes words with double letters (miSS aNNa grEEn). So she likes coFFEE and swiMMing and bEEf and fEEt and aPPles and chEEse.

Answer questions from the class with short answers.

Student B Does she like wine?
You No, she doesn't.
Student C Does she like beer? (bEEr)
You Yes, she does.

You can help them.
Student D Does she like blue?
You No, she doesn't like blue. But she likes yellow and green.

ACTIVITY NINE

Unit twenty-five. Student A

Tell Student B about your picture.

Student A It's going to rain in my picture.
Student B It isn't going to rain in my picture.

Talk about:

the son	the mother
the grandmother	the father
the daughter	the dog
the grandfather	

ACTIVITY TEN

Unit twenty-six. Student A

This is a picture of your desk yesterday. Student B has got a picture of your desk today. The office cleaner is very tidy. Everything is in a different place.

Ask Student B five questions.
Yesterday, the keys were on the desk. Where are they now?

Answer Student B's questions.

YESTERDAY

ACTIVITY ELEVEN

Unit two. Student B

Ask student A.
Can you spell (goodbye)?

Say *You're right* **or** *You're wrong.*

ACTIVITY TWELVE

Unit five. Student B

With Student A look at Student A's pictures for ten seconds.
Close your book. Ask Student A questions.

Student A	Picture one.
Student B	Are they (watches)?
Student A	Yes, they are. / No, they aren't.

With Student A look at your pictures for ten seconds.
Then answer Student A's questions.

Student B	Picture one.
Student A	Are they (umbrellas)?
Student B	Yes, they are. / No, they aren't.

ACTIVITY THIRTEEN

Unit nine. Student B

This is your room. Describe your room to Student A.

Find the different things.
Ask Student A questions about his / her picture.

Is there (a television)?
Are there any (oranges)?
What colour is (the telephone)?
What colour are (the walls)?

ACTIVITY FOURTEEN

Unit ten. Student B

Ask about Student A's pictures. Make notes.

jacket	size	colour	how much
shorts	size	colour	how much
skirt	size	colour	how much
shoes	size	colour	how much

M – $69.49
38 – $94.95
S – $59.99
XL – $95.50

Answer Student A's questions.

ACTIVITY FIFTEEN

Unit sixteen. Student B

You are at the station. Ask Student A for directions to these places.
the central car park
the church
the supermarket
Burger Land

Give Student B directions to these places.
the hospital
the bank
the post office
the ABC cinema

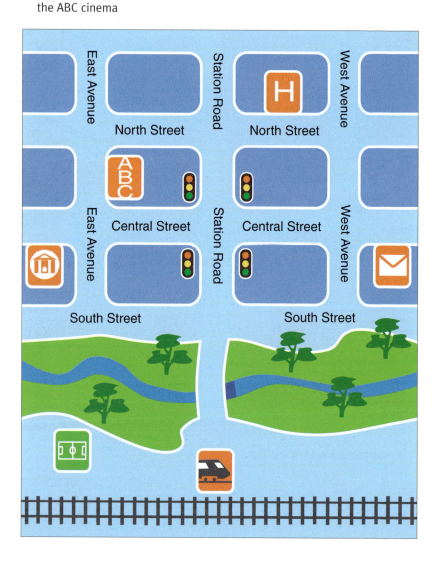

ACTIVITY SIXTEEN

Unit twenty. Student B

Student A has a diary from Monday 21st to Sunday 27th August.
Ask Student A questions and make an appointment with Ms Cooper.

Look at the diary. You are Mr Freeman's secretary.
Student A wants an appointment.

MONDAY 11 FEBRUARY

morning	Dentist 9.00
	9.45 – 10.00 Miss Melville
	10.00 – 11.00 Mr Hawthorne
lunch	11.00 – 12.30 Mrs Twain
afternoon	2.00 – 5.00 Ms James
	Finish 5.00
evening	Dinner, Ms James

TUESDAY 12 FEBRUARY

morning	8.00 – 10.00 computer training
	10.00 – 12.00 Japanese lesson
	11.00 – 12.30 Mr Pound
lunch	No appointments, please.
afternoon	
evening	Finish 5.30

WEDNESDAY 13 FEBRUARY

morning	8.30 – 9.30 interview new secretaries
	9.45 – 12.00 Free
lunch	Mr Norris
afternoon	No appointments please
evening	Finish 7.00

THURSDAY 14 FEBRUARY

morning	8.30 – 9.15 Miss Steinbeck
	9.15 – 10.15 Mr Fitzgerald
	10.15 – 12.30 Mrs Mailer
lunch	12.30 – 2.00 Mr Bellow
afternoon	2.15 – 4.00 Dr Williams
	4.00 – 5.00 Free
evening	Finish 5.00

FRIDAY 15 FEBRUARY

morning	8.30 – 10.00 Mrs Dickinson
	10.00 – 11.00 Mr Whitman
	11.00 – 12.30 Mr Pound
lunch	Free
afternoon	2.00 – 3.00 Free
	Finish early today 3.00
evening	

SATURDAY 16 FEBRUARY

Not at work

SUNDAY 17 FEBRUARY

Taxi 7.30. Check in 9.55
Fly to Tokyo, 11.55 BA 005

ACTIVITY SEVENTEEN

Unit twenty-one. Student B

Find these in your picture:

the young man   the businessman
the boy   the old man and the old woman
the girl   the dog
the young woman

Student A's picture has got the same people. Ask about them.
What is the young man doing?

Then answer Student A's questions about your picture.

ACTIVITY EIGHTEEN

Unit twenty-four. All the other students

Read the puzzle.
Miss Anna Green likes coffee, but she doesn't like tea.
She really loves swimming, but she really hates the sea.
She enjoys eating beef, but she doesn't like meat.
She hates people's hands, but she loves their feet.
Does she like apples? Does she like cheese?
I can tell you the answer if you say please.

What things does she like? Ask Student A questions with *Does she like ... ?* until you guess the rule. When you guess, don't tell the class. Help Student A.

ACTIVITY NINETEEN

Unit twenty-five. Student B

Listen to Student A. How is your picture different?

Tell student A about your picture.

Student A It's going to rain in my picture.
Student B It isn't going to rain in my picture.

Talk about:

the son	the mother
the grandmother	the father
the daughter	the dog
the grandfather	

ACTIVITY TWENTY

Unit twenty-six. Student B

This is a picture of Student A's desk today. Student A has got a picture of the same desk yesterday. The office cleaner is very tidy. Everything is in a different place.

Answer student A's questions.

Ask Student A five questions.

The keys are on the chair now. Where were they yesterday?

TODAY

ACTIVITY TWENTY-ONE

Extension twenty-eight

Last year (1) .... had a holiday in (2) .... On her first day, she had a swim in the hotel swimming pool. It was very hot so at (3) .... she had a (4) .... and a (5) .... ice-cream. On (6) .... the sky was (7) ...., so she had (8) .... in her room. On her last day the hotel had a party. She had a dance with (9) .... He was (10) .... and very handsome. They had a good time.

TRANSCRIPT

🔊 1.9
Man What's her number?
Woman Maria?
Man Mm hmm.
Woman Her number's 01865 636442.

🔊 1.10
Man What's my mobile phone number? I don't know!
Woman Your number's 07968 251033.

🔊 1.11
Woman Mike, what's your fax number?
Man 024 7628 9135.

🔊 1.12
Rob Hi! My name's Rob.
Anna Hi, Rob.
Rob Um, what's your name?
Anna My name's Anna.
Rob OK, Anna. What's your telephone number?
Anna My number's 01207 395684.

🔊 1.17
He's a cleaner.
His name's Mr Wilson.
She's a scientist.
Her name's Miss Clark.
She's a shop assistant.
Her name's Mrs Carter.
He's a doctor.
His name's Dr Green.

🔊 1.21
Tony Hello, hello, and welcome to 'Can you spell?' Thank you! Thank you! Contestant number one, what's your name?
Watson Watson. Philip Watson.
Tony OK, Mr Watson ...
Watson Er. My name's Dr Watson.
Tony Sorry?
Watson My name isn't Mr Watson. My name's Dr Watson.
Tony Are you a medical doctor?
Watson No, I'm not a medical doctor.
Tony Oh? What's your job, Dr Watson?
Watson I'm a scientist. At Oxford University.
Tony So, contestant number one is Dr Philip Watson, a scientist at Oxford University.

Tony And contestant number two, what's your name?
Smith Tracy Smith.
Tony Miss Smith or Mrs Smith?
Smith Mrs Smith.
Tony And what's your job, Mrs Smith?
Smith Sorry?
Tony What's your job, Tracy?
Smith I'm a cleaner.
Tony OK. Dr Watson is a scientist, and Mrs Smith is a cleaner. Question number one. Can you spell 'journalist'?

Tony Dr Watson?
Watson J-O-U-R-N-E-L-I-S-T.
Tony Oh, sorry, Dr Watson. That's wrong. Tracy, can you spell 'journalist'?
Smith Um, I don't know. Um ...
Tony Five seconds ... five, four, three, two ...
Smith Er, J-O-U-R-N-A-L-I-S-T. Journalist.
Tony That's right!

🔊 1.22
Man What's her first name?
Woman Lucia.
Man What's her family name?
Woman Rodrigues.
Man Is she married?
Woman No, she isn't. She's single.
Man What's her job?
Woman She's a student.
Man Where's she from?
Woman She's from Brazil.

🔊 1.24
Miss Lucia Rodrigues Brazil Brazilian
Dr Karl Brandt Germany German
Mrs Maria Lopez Spain Spanish
Mr Paul Lefort France French
Ms Miki Tanaka Japan Japanese

🔊 1.27
Woman Hello! How are you?
Man I'm fine, thanks. And you?
Woman Fine, thanks.

🔊 1.34
Woman 1 Ow!
Man Oh, I'm sorry.

🔊 1.35
Woman 1 Um, excuse me ...
Woman 2 Yes?

🔊 1.36
Woman Are you English?
Man Yes.

🔊 1.37
Man Excuse me ...
Woman Sorry.

🔊 1.38
Man Do you speak French?
Woman Sorry?
Man Do you speak French?
Woman No.

🔊 1.39
Woman Um, excuse me?
Man Yes. Can I help you?

TRANSCRIPT

1.40
Woman Bill!
Man What?
Woman The phone. For you.

1.41
Jack Maria?
Maria Yes?
Jack I'm Jack Green.
Maria Ah, yes. Jack. Er, sorry …

1.44
eleven
nineteen
thirteen
sixteen
twelve
seventeen
twenty
fourteen
ten
fifteen
eighteen

1.45
one — a backpack
two — a towel
three — an apple
four — a map
five — a phone
six — an orange
seven — an identity card
eight — a dictionary
nine — a camera
ten — a pen
eleven — a key
twelve — a passport
thirteen — a toothbrush
fourteen — an envelope
fifteen — a penknife
sixteen — a watch
seventeen — a film
eighteen — an umbrella
nineteen — a ticket
twenty — a hat

1.46
Man What are they?
Woman They're films.

1.47
Woman Are they your keys?
Man No, they aren't.

1.48
Woman 1 They're toothbrushes.
Woman 2 Sorry. Can you repeat that?
Woman 1 Yes. Toothbrushes.

1.49
Woman What are 'aspirins' in English?
Man They're aspirins.
Woman No, what are they in English?
Man Aspirins.
Woman Oh!

1.50
Woman Are they envelopes?
Man Yes, they are.

1.51
maps
tickets
hats
backpacks
passports
envelopes
cameras
keys
aspirins
pens
films
identity cards
umbrellas
towels
dictionaries
watches
toothbrushes
oranges

1.60
thirteen   G seventy
A ninety   H fifteen
B eighteen   I sixty
C forty   J fourteen
D thirty   K seventeen
E fifty   L eighty
F sixteen

1.64
Server Next.
Customer Hi. A cheeseburger, uh, and … and fries. And a chocolate shake.
Server Eat in or take out?
Customer Eat in.
Server That's five fifty, please.
Customer Here you are. Thank you.
Server You're welcome.

1.65
Server And the next, please.
Customer A hot dog, a salad, and a cola.
Server Is that a regular or a large cola?
Customer Er, large.
Server Eat in or take out?
Customer Take out.
Server OK. Six twenty.
Customer Sorry? It's five twenty.
Server Oh, yes. Sorry. It's my first day. I'm new here.
Customer OK.

1.66
Server Good morning. What would you like?
Customer Um, let's see, um …
Server Yes?
Customer Well, um, yes, fish. Fish burger and … um, fries.
Server Fish and fries? Anything to drink?
Customer Oh, drink. Yes. Um, a straw… no. Er. Just a mineral water, please.
Server Fish and fries and a mineral water?
Customer Yes. That's right.
Server Are you going to eat in or take out?
Customer Oh, um … eat in, I think. Yes. Eat in.
Server Five thirty.
Customer Two, and one is three, and one is four, and one is five … five. And … ten … twenty … thirty.
Server Thanks.

TRANSCRIPT

✱ 1.71

twenty-seven	a hot tap
twenty-eight	a big car
twenty-nine	new shoes
thirty	a cold tap
thirty-one	a small car
thirty-two	old shoes

✱ 1.72

... and Wales are in **red** shirts, and England are in **white** shirts. And it's Jones at number six for Wales ... Jones to Bevan ... Bevan to Morgan. Morgan's **fast**, very **fast**. And here's Kevin Smith for England. Oh! Morgan's down. He's **hurt**. And it's a **yellow** card for Smith! And Morgan's up, and he's an angry man, a very **angry** man. Oh! Smith's down. He's **hurt**. Morgan's a very **young** player. He's **crazy**! And the **French** referee is there. Is it a **yellow** card or a red card? Oh! It's a **red** card for the Welsh player! He's off, and that's bad for Wales!

✱ 1.76

A Room thirteen thirty, please.
B The keys to forty fourteen, please.
C Can I have the keys to seventeen seventy?
D I'm in room fifteen fifty-five.
E Is that room nineteen nineteen?
F May I have the keys to eighteen eighty?
G My room number's sixteen oh six.
H I think her number's twelve twenty.

✱ 1.77

There are two double beds in the room. There are two small lights on the wall. There's a white telephone and a radio. There's a table and there are two chairs. There's an armchair. There's a wardrobe. There's a colour television. There's a picture on the wall. There's a blue carpet on the floor.

✱ 1.78

Man Where are the lights?
Woman They're on the wall.
Man Are there any towels?
Woman No, there aren't. Are there any chairs?
Man Yes, there are.
Woman Are the beds double or single?
Man They're double beds.

✱ 1.82

Woman Can I help you?
Man Yes, I'm looking for some trainers.
Woman For him or for her?
Man Sorry?
Woman Who are they for? Him or her?
Man For him, please.
Woman What size?
Man Thirty-four.
Woman What colour?
Man White.
Woman OK. Take a seat.

✱ 1.83

Woman We're looking for some shoes. Size thirty-nine.
Man Right. Are they for you or for her?
Woman They're for her.
Man What colour?
Woman Black. They're for school.

✱ 1.84

Man I'm looking for a grey T-shirt.
Woman Yes, sir. What size?
Man I don't know. Large or extra large.
Woman Is it for you?
Man Yes, it's for me.
Woman Hmm. Extra large, I think.

✱ 1.85

Woman I'm looking for a light-grey sweatshirt.
Man Yes, ma'am. Er, what size are you?
Woman Oh, it isn't for me!
Man Who is it for?
Woman It's for my mother.
Man What size is she?
Woman I don't know. Medium or large.
Man Here's a large sweatshirt.
Woman Hmm. No. Medium, then.

✱ 1.86

A credit card	G stamps
B identity card	H matches
C driving licence	I sunglasses
D pen	J keys
E comb	K paper hankies
F calculator	L sweets

✱ 1.90

Woman Have you got an EU passport, a European Union passport?
Man No, I haven't. I've got a Japanese passport.
Woman OK, here's a landing card for you.
Man Thank you. Oh, excuse me, I haven't got a pen ...

✱ 1.91

Bouncer Just a minute, miss ...
Woman Yes?
Bouncer Are you over twenty-one?
Woman Yes!
Bouncer Have you got an ID card?
Woman I've got my driving licence.

✱ 1.92

Woman Have you got two tickets for tonight, please?
Man Yes, we have. Cash or credit card?
Woman Credit card.
Man What card have you got?
Woman American Express.

TRANSCRIPT

1.93

Man Mum, have you got three coins?
Woman Here you are.
Man Thanks, Mum.
Woman Just a minute. Have you got a comb?
Man Oh, Mum ...

2.07

Mother Eat your breakfast, Benny.
Mother Don't forget your lunch.
Traffic signal Don't walk.
Driver Sit down, kids.
Teacher Be quiet! Don't talk. Benny, don't look at them. Look at me.
Teacher Be careful, Benny!
Driver Don't stand up. Sit there.
Mother Say 'please.'
Mother Say 'Thank you.'
Mother Turn off the TV, Benny.
Mother Give me the comic. Turn off the light.
Mother Sweet Dreams.

2.08

Close your eyes. Don't open them! Write your first name on the paper. Don't write your family name. Write your teacher's name. Write this phone number: seven six eight, four three five two. Don't open your eyes! Draw a man. Draw a woman. Open your eyes. Look at your picture. Look at your partner's picture.

2.09

Student A: Listen, and follow the instructions.
Stand up. Go to the door. Open the door. Close the door. Go to your chair. Sit down. Thank you.

2.10

Student B: Listen, and follow the instructions.
Close your book. Look at your partner. Look at the door. Look at your teacher. Stand up. Sit down. Stand up. Sit down. Don't stand up. Thank you.

2.11

Student C: Listen, and follow the instructions.
Stand up. Go to the door. Open the door. Say 'Goodbye'. Go out. Stop! Don't go! Come in. Close the door. Thank you.

2.13

My name's Jade Butler, and I live in Southend. I don't work in Southend. I work in London. I'm a receptionist and I work in a hospital.

2.14

William Hello, I'm William. What's your name?
Jade Jade.
William Do you live in London, Jade?
Jade No, I don't.
William Do you work in London?
Jade Yes, I do.
William What's your job?
Jade I'm a receptionist.
William Oh, do you work in a hotel?
Jade No, I don't. I work in a hospital.

2.15

Jade Butler lives in Southend. She lives in a flat. She doesn't work in Southend. She works in London. She's a receptionist and she works in a hospital.

2.16

Woman Does she live in London?
Man No, she doesn't.
Woman Does she work in London?
Man Yes, she does.

2.21

Monday	Friday
Tuesday	Saturday
Wednesday	Sunday
Thursday	

2.22

Man What time does the post office open?
Woman It opens at nine o'clock.
Man Thanks.

2.23

Woman Oh, no. It's closed! And it's only four fifty-five!
Man No, it isn't. Your watch is wrong. It's five o'clock.
Woman But I haven't got any money!
Man It's OK. There's a twenty-four hour cash machine.

2.24

Man We haven't got any milk.
Woman No, but that's OK. Tesco's open.
Man It's eleven o'clock at night!
Woman It's open twenty-four hours a day.

2.25

Woman Excuse me, is there a Tourist Information Centre near here?
Man Tourist Information? Yes, there is. It's over there.
Woman Thank you very much.
Man But it isn't open.
Woman Sorry?
Man It isn't open. It's Sunday. It doesn't open on Sundays.

TRANSCRIPT

✱ 2.26
This is Smith and Jones Limited. We are sorry, our offices are closed. Our office hours are from nine a.m. to six p.m., Monday to Friday. Please leave a message after the tone.

✱ 2.27
Woman 1 Can we go shopping this evening?
Woman 2 Oh, yes. It's Thursday. There's late shopping tonight. The shops close at eight o'clock.

✱ 2.28
Man 1 What time is it?
Man 2 Ten forty-five.
Man 1 I'd like a drink.
Man 2 Me too. What time does the pub open?
Man 1 At eleven.
Man 2 Good.

✱ 2.29
This is a recorded message. These offices are open to the public from nine to five, Monday to Friday. Please telephone again during these hours.

✱ 2.30
Man Is the library open or closed today?
Woman It's Wednesday. It's closed.

✱ 2.37
Man Double espresso, please.
Woman That's one fifty, please.
Man Thanks. Um, is there a cinema near here?
Woman Yes, there's a cinema in Dorset Road.
Man Can you give me directions?
Woman Yes, this café's in Lord Street, OK? Go along Lord Street, and turn … um … right into the High Street. Go along the High Street, across the Town Square, past the town hall. Go to the end of the High Street. There's a park at the end of the High Street. Turn right. That's East Street. Go along East Street. Go across the bridge. Then South Road is on the right … it's the third on the right, I think. Anyway, go along South Road, and turn first left into Dorset Road. The cinema's on the left.
Man I'm sorry?

✱ 2.38
Tim Hello.
Bob Hi, Tim. It's me, Bob.
Tim Bob! Great to hear you. Where are you?
Bob I'm in town on business. Are you busy today?
Tim No.
Bob Great. Er, can we meet for coffee?
Tim Yes, come here for coffee.
Bob I haven't got your address. Where do you live?
Tim Fifteen, Dorset Road.
Bob Can you give me directions?
Tim Yes, sure. Where are you now?
Bob I'm in a phone box at the railway station.
Tim Can you see South Road?
Bob Yes.
Tim OK. Um, go along South Road. Dorset Road is the second on the left. Go past the pub. Go across New Road. Burger Land's on your right. Number fifteen's on the left. My flat's on the first floor.
Bob OK. See you soon.
Tim See you.

✱ 2.39
Ms Blair Ah, Suzy! There you are.
Suzy Good morning, Ms Blair.
Ms Blair I've got some jobs for you.
Suzy Yes, Ms Blair.
Ms Blair Go to the post office and buy some stamps …
Suzy First class or second class stamps?
Ms Blair First class. One hundred first class stamps.
Suzy OK …
Ms Blair And go to the bank. Ask for some small change. We haven't got any.
Suzy OK …
Ms Blair And go to the supermarket. We haven't got any coffee for the office. Oh, and some sugar.
Suzy OK …
Ms Blair And here are some photos of the town. Give them to Mr Taylor at the tourist information office. Here's some money. Oh, dear. It's raining. Take an umbrella.

✱ 2.42
Hi, I'm Ricky Cooper. I work in a factory in San Diego, California. The factory produces silicon chips for computers. I get up early, at five thirty. I don't have breakfast at home. I have breakfast in the factory canteen. That's at six thirty. And then I work from seven to three thirty. I stop and have lunch from eleven thirty to twelve. I don't have a coffee break, but there's a coffee machine. I have dinner at six, and I go to bed at nine thirty.

✱ 2.45
Attendant Would you like another drink with your meal?
Tony Yes, please.

TRANSCRIPT

Katie No, thanks. Not for me.
Tony Yes, you would, Katie. It's free.
Katie No, I wouldn't, Tony.
Tony Yes, she'd like some champagne, please.
Katie Oh, all right.
Attendant Which starter would you like?
Tony I'd like ham with melon, please.
Attendant For you, madam?
Katie Um, green salad for me.
Attendant Which main course would you like?
Tony I'd like chicken with rice.
Katie And I'd like Scottish salmon with potatoes and peas.
Attendant OK, chicken and fish. Which dessert would you like?
Tony I'd like some chocolate cake. Katie?
Katie Oh, not for me, thank you.
Attendant Would you like tea or coffee?
Tony Coffee, please.
Attendant Would she like some coffee?
Tony No, she wouldn't, thank you. She's asleep.

✱ 2.46
Attendant Would you like a newspaper?
Katie Yes, please. What have you got?
Attendant We've got *The Times* or *USA Today*.
Katie I'd like *The Times*, please.

✱ 2.47
Attendant Would you like some tea?
Katie No, thanks. Have you got any coffee?
Attendant Yes, just a minute.

✱ 2.51
Kevin Can you help me, Claire?
Claire Yeah, OK. What's this?
Kevin It's a registration form … it's for the employment agency.
Claire Right. Show me. Can you drive? That's easy. Tick 'yes'. Have you got an HGV licence? Well, have you got an HGV licence?
Kevin I don't know. What's that?
Claire HGV … Heavy Goods Vehicle. Can you drive a truck, Kevin?
Kevin No, I can't.
Claire Well, tick 'no', then. Um. Can you speak a foreign language?
Kevin No, I can't.
Claire Yes, you can!
Kevin No, I can't.
Claire What's French for 'yes'?
Kevin Er …
Claire Oh, come on! It's easy, Kevin.
Kevin Is it 'oui'?

Claire That's right. Tick 'yes', and write 'French.'
Kevin OK.
Claire What's Spanish for 'yes'?
Kevin Oh, yeah. I know that. It's 'Si'.
Claire Yeah! Put 'Spanish' and 'Italian'.
Kevin Italian?
Claire Right. Si. That's 'yes' in Italian and Spanish. And pizza, spaghetti bolognese, pasta, capucinno, espresso … You know them. What's next?
Kevin Computer skills.
Claire Have you got any?
Kevin I can use an Xbox and a PlayStation.
Claire Can you type?
Kevin I can type with one finger.
Claire OK. Tick 'yes'. Can you use a PC?
Kevin Yes.
Claire A word-processor?
Kevin Er … uh …
Claire Put 'yes'. A spreadsheet?
Kevin What's a spreadsheet?
Claire Put 'no.' What job would you like, Kevin?
Kevin Er … a rock star.

✱ 2.52
Valentine's Day is the 14th of February.
Christmas Day is the 25th of December.
New Year's Day is the 1st of January.
American Independence Day is the 4th of July.

✱ 2.53
January	July
February	August
March	September
April	October
May	November
June	December

✱ 2.58
Receptionist How are you today, Mrs Adams?
Woman Fine, thanks. Can I make an appointment for next week?
Receptionist Of course. When for?
Woman Er. Thursday morning.
Receptionist Is nine o'clock OK?
Woman It's very early. Has she got an appointment at eleven or twelve?
Receptionist Urm. How about eleven fifteen?
Woman Yes, that's fine.
Receptionist Good. Thursday the thirtieth at eleven fifteen.
Woman Thank you. Can you call me a taxi?
Receptionist Of course. Take a seat over there.
Woman Thank you.

TRANSCRIPT

✱ 2.59
Man Excuse me?
Receptionist Yes?
Man Can I make an appointment with Dr Smith for next Tuesday?
Receptionist What name?
Man Darren Morley.
Receptionist What time?
Man Any time. I'm free all day. I can't work at the moment. Not with my leg.
Receptionist Um. Eleven forty-five?
Man Yeah, OK.
Receptionist That's Tuesday the twenty-eighth of July at eleven forty-five with Dr Smith.
Man Thanks.

✱ 2.60
Receptionist Yes?
Woman I'd like an appointment with the nurse, please.
Receptionist For you or for her?
Woman For her. It's for a vaccination.
Receptionist What's her name?
Woman Isobel. Isobel Patton.
Receptionist Right. The nurse is here on Tuesdays and Fridays.
Woman Um, Friday, I think. Is she free this Friday?
Receptionist I'm afraid not. Next Friday. That's the thirty-first of July.
Woman Fine. Is she free in the afternoon?
Receptionist Er, she's free at four thirty.
Woman That's great. Thank you.

✱ 2.61
Receptionist Can I help you, Mr Atkins?
Man Er, yes. Yes, please. Can I make an appointment with Dr Wilson?
Receptionist When for?
Man Tomorrow.
Receptionist I'm afraid she's busy tomorrow. Is Friday the twenty-fourth OK?
Man No. I'm busy on Friday. Can I see Dr Smith?
Receptionist Tomorrow?
Man That's right. Tomorrow.
Receptionist Dr Smith's busy tomorrow. He hasn't got any free appointments.
Man Oh. How about Saturday morning?
Receptionist Yes, he's here on Saturday morning. What time?
Man Is ten o'clock OK?
Receptionist He's free at nine fifty.
Man That's fine.
Receptionist All right. Saturday the twenty-fifth at nine fifty.
Man Thank you very much.

✱ 2.63
Dad 543 7862.
Tracy Dad! Can you video *Neighbours* for me?
Dad No, I can't, Tracy! I'm busy.
Tracy What are you doing?
Dad I'm having a shower!

✱ 2.64
Mum Yes?
Tracy Mum? I can't watch *Neighbours*.
Mum Why not? What are you doing?
Tracy I'm working late. Can you video it?
Mum Oh, no. Sorry, Tracy. I'm shopping.

✱ 2.65
Pete Hello?
Tracy Hi, is Dave there?
Pete Yes, he is.
Tracy Can I speak to him?
Pete No, I'm afraid you can't.
Tracy Why not? What's he doing?
Pete He's sleeping.

✱ 2.66
Jordan Jordan Maxwell.
Tracy Jordan?
Jordan Hi, Tracy.
Tracy Are you at home?
Jordan No. I'm with Alice. We're sitting on a plane. We're about to …
Attendant You can't use your mobile phone now, sir. The plane's taking off.

✱ 2.67
Ellen Hello. This is Ellen speaking …
Tracy Hi, Ellen? Are you watching *Neighbours*?
Ellen Yeah, I am. It's great.
Tracy Can you video it for me?
Ellen Oh, no, sorry, Trace. I can't. I haven't got a videotape.

✱ 2.69
Debbie Are you going on holiday this year?
Mark Yes, I'm going to Italy.
Debbie Really? Where to?
Mark Rimini.
Debbie That's nice.
Mark Rimini's very popular.
Debbie Yes, I know. When are you going?
Mark August.
Debbie Oh, really? Italy's lovely in August. Very hot.

✱ 2.71
Debbie Hello, Mrs Baxter.
Mrs Baxter Hello, Debbie.
Debbie What would you like today?
Mrs Baxter A shampoo, cut and blow dry.
Debbie Right. How's your neighbour, Mrs Lester?

TRANSCRIPT

Mrs Baxter She's in hospital. She's having an operation on Monday.
Debbie Oh, I am sorry. How's your little dog? All right?
Mrs Baxter No, he isn't very well. I'm taking him to the vet this afternoon.
Debbie Oh, dear. Poor thing. How's Mr Baxter?
Mrs Baxter He's got the flu.
Debbie Oh, no.
Mrs Baxter He's seeing the doctor tomorrow. He's sneezing all the time.
Debbie That's awful.
Mrs Baxter Yes …

✻ 2.72

Debbie Hello, Mrs Baxter.
Mrs Baxter Hello, Debbie.
Debbie What would you like today?
Mrs Baxter A shampoo, cut and blow dry.
Debbie Right. How's your neighbour, Mrs Lester?
Mrs Baxter She's in hospital. She's having an operation on Monday.
Debbie How's your little dog? All right?
Mrs Baxter No, he isn't very well. I'm taking him to the vet this afternoon.
Debbie Poor thing. How's Mr Baxter?
Mrs Baxter He's got the flu.
Debbie
Mrs Baxter He's seeing the doctor tomorrow. He's sneezing all the time.
Debbie
Mrs Baxter Yes …

✻ 2.76

Woman 1 James Carter's on the phone.
Woman 2 Ergh, not James Carter!

✻ 2.77

Man Jack Douglas and Lucy Ford are in that new film at the Odeon. How about seeing it?
Woman I don't know. I like him, but I don't like her.

✻ 2.78

Man 1 Let's get some popcorn.
Man 2 Yeah. Popcorn! Great!

✻ 2.79

Woman Oh, turn that music off.
Man It's number one this week.
Woman Well, it's awful!

✻ 2.80

Man 1 There's someone at the door.
Man 2 Oh yeah. It's Maria! Maria!

✻ 2.87

Woman Titanic's my favourite film!
Man Is it good?
Woman Yeah. Brilliant!

✻ 2.88

Woman The ship's going to sink. It's very sad.
Man Oh, dear. When?
Woman At the end.

✻ 2.89

Woman They aren't going to get married.
Man Why not?
Woman Because she …
Man No, don't tell me.

✻ 2.90

Woman They're going to fall in love.
Man Shhh!
Woman Sorry.

✻ 2.91

Woman They're going to jump!
Man Please … be quiet! Don't tell me the story!

✻ 2.92

Woman He's going to die!
Man Huh. I'm not going to go to the cinema with you again. This is the last time!

✻ 2.93

Woman It's going to rain.
Man She's going to have a baby.
Woman They're going to get married.
Man She's going to jump.
Woman She's going to have a shower.
Man They're going to be late.

✻ 2.94

There's five point six million in the jackpot this Saturday night. First ball out is … number forty-five. And next is number nine. The third one tonight is thirty, and we're waiting for a fourth. Seven. Next is number fourteen. And the sixth one for this Saturday night is number twenty-seven.

✻ 2.95

So tonight's winning lottery numbers again, this time in ascending order: Seven. Nine. Fourteen. Twenty-seven. Thirty. Forty-five.

✻ 3.09

Woman Monsieur Lefort?
Man Yes?
Woman I'm your chauffeur, sir. From V.I.P. Cars.
Man Thanks for meeting me.
Woman How was the train journey?
Man It wasn't bad.

TRANSCRIPT

Woman How long was it?
Man Three hours.
Woman That's a long time. Was there a restaurant on the train?
Man Yes, there was a buffet.
Woman How was the food?
Man Oh, it was OK.
Woman And what was the weather like in Paris?
Man Ah, it was hot and sunny.
Woman Well, I'm sorry, it's cold and cloudy here in London. The car's outside. Can I help you with your bags?
Man No, thank you. I can carry them.

3.10
My last holiday was in the summer. I was in Cornwall in England with some friends. We were camping. The weather was wonderful. We were on the beach every day. The food was very good. There was a good fish restaurant near the campsite, and there were three pubs in the village.

3.12
Yesterday was a holiday. They had a family lunch. They had lunch outside. The parents don't usually have lunch with their children, but they had lunch with them yesterday. They had steak, salad and a bottle of red wine.

3.13
They had lunch at 12.30 in front of the TV. They usually have lunch at school on weekdays but yesterday was a holiday. They had a takeaway. They had burgers, fries and milkshakes.

3.14
Yesterday was a special lunch. They had a family celebration. They don't usually have lunch together. They had chicken and pasta. They had wine with their meal. They don't usually have wine with lunch.

3.15
He had his lunch at 1 p.m in a restaurant. He had rice, fish and tea. He had lunch alone. He usually has lunch alone.

3.32
Interviewer Happy birthday, Herbert.
Herbert Eh?
Interviewer Happy birthday. You're a hundred years old today. That's a great achievement.
Herbert Oh, yes, I'm a hundred.
Interviewer Where were you born?
Herbert I was born in Oxford. I had four brothers and six sisters.
Interviewer What was your father's job?
Herbert My old dad was a train driver.
Interviewer Did you go to school in Oxford?
Herbert Oh, yes. I went to school in Oxford. I was clever. I passed all the exams, but my parents didn't have any money. So I got a job when I was twelve. I worked in a shop.
Interviewer How long did you work there?
Herbert Oh, not long. Two years. I didn't like it. Then I got a job on the railway with my old dad.
Interviewer When did you get married?
Herbert Seventy-five years ago. I met my first wife on holiday in Southsea. I was twenty-two.
Interviewer Was she on holiday too?
Herbert No, she lived there. So I moved to Southsea when we got married. And I got a job there. I was a bus driver for forty years. We had two children, a boy and a girl. And now I've got six grandchildren, and eleven great-grandchildren, and fourteen great-great-grandchildren.
Interviewer Do you know all their names?
Herbert Oh, no. I can't remember them all. I'm getting old. I'm a hundred today, you know.
Interviewer And are they coming to see you today?
Herbert Oh, yes, I think so. And we're going out to dinner. Me and my wife.
Interviewer Your wife?
Herbert My second wife. My first wife died twenty years ago. I got married again last year.
Interviewer You got married again at ninety nine?
Herbert Oh, yes. She's younger than me … she's only eighty-eight. I'm a lucky man. I'm a hundred today, you know.
Interviewer Yes. Happy birthday, Herbert.

Extension 28: The year 1000
The sentences are all true.

Extension 30. Twentieth century faces
A: 4, 5, 6, 11
B: 1, 9, 10, 14, 16
C: 2, 8, 13, 17
D: 3, 7, 12, 15

GRAMMAR

Articles

Indefinite articles: *a /an*
Definite article: *the*

consonants	b, c, d, f, g, h, j, k, l, m, n, p, q, r, s, t, v, w, x, (y), z
vowels	a, e, i, o, u, (y)

Use *a* before the <u>sound</u> of a consonant.
 a pen, a bus, a nice apple

Use *an* before the <u>sound</u> of a vowel.
 an apple, an egg, an ice-cream, an orange, an umbrella, an old man

Remember that the important thing is sound, not spelling.
So we say: *a union, a European* because the sound is 'y'.
We say: *an honest person, an hour* because the 'h' is silent.

Adjectives

Adjectives don't change for number or person.
 *a **big** book   **big** books*
 *He's **angry**.   She's **angry**.   They're **angry**.*

Adjectives usually come before nouns.
 He's got a new watch. NOT *He's got a watch new.*

Determiners

'Determiners' include other grammatical areas.
Here are some examples of determiners.

articles	the, a, an
demonstratives	this, that, these, those
possessive adjectives	my, your, his, her, their, our
quantifiers	some, any, one, three

Genitives

Gentives are the possessive form of nouns.
 He's Anna's husband.
 That's Mr Smith's newspaper.

Names ending in *-s*. We can use:
 She's Charles' girlfriend. OR *She's Charles's girlfriend.*

GRAMMAR

Nouns: singular and plural

	Regular plurals			Irregular plurals	
singular	key	apple	watch	man	woman
plural	keys	apples	watches	men	women

Pronouns and possessive adjectives

Subject pronouns	I	you	he	she	it	we	they
Object pronouns	me	you	him	her	it	us	them
Possessive adjectives	my	your	his	her	its	our	their

Subject pronouns and object pronouns

I / You / We / They	know	him. / her. / it. / me.
He / She / It	knows	you. / us. / them.

Possessive adjectives

What	's / is	my / your / her / his / our / their	name? / job? / nationality?
	're / are	your / our / their	names? / jobs?

Indefinite pronouns

There	is	something / nothing	on the table.
There	isn't	anything	on the table.

Is	there	anything	on the table?

GRAMMAR

Prepositions

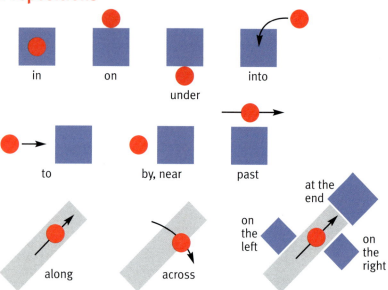

Some / any

See **be: there is ... / there are ...** in VERBS on p.216.

Time words

at	on	in
at 6 o'clock	on Tuesday	in the afternoon
at 7.30	on 12th May	in September
at night	on Christmas Day	in the summer
		in 2002

from 6 o'clock **to** 6.30
five days **ago**

Past	Present	Future
then	now	then
yesterday	today	tomorrow
yesterday morning	this (morning)	tomorrow morning
last week	this week	next week
last month	this month	next month
last year	this year	next year

GRAMMAR

Verbs

Imperatives

Positive

Stop! Listen.	
Be	careful. quiet.
Turn on Turn off	the T.V. the tap.
Go Come	home. to the door.

Negative

Don't	stop. go. look.	
	be	stupid. late.
	turn on turn off	the TV. the light.

Be

be, present tense

Positive and negative

I	'm / am / 'm not / am not	from London. British. late.
He She It	's / is / isn't / 's not / is not	
You We They	are / 're / aren't / 're not / are not	

Questions

Am	I	late?
Is	he she it	British? from London?
Are	you we they	

Short answers

Yes, I am. / No, I'm not.
Yes, he is. / No, he isn't.
Yes, she is. / No, she isn't.
Yes, it is. / No, it isn't.
Yes, you are. / No, you aren't.
Yes, we are. / No, we aren't.
Yes, they are. / No, they aren't.

GRAMMAR

be: there is ... / there are ...

Positive

There	is	a	bed. table.
		an	office. armchair.
	are	some	towels. lights.

Negative

There	isn't	a	bed. table.
		an	office. armchair.
	aren't	any	towels. lights.

Questions

Is	there	a	bed? table?
		an	office? armchair?
Are		any	towels? lights?

Short answers

Yes, there is.
No, there isn't.

Yes, there are.
No, there aren't.

Present continuous tense

Positive and negative

I	'm am 'm not am not	having	breakfast. a bath.
He She It	's is isn't 's not is not	going	to France. to work.
You We They	're are aren't 're not are not	sleeping. eating.	

Questions

Am	I	having	breakfast? a bath?
Is	he she it	going	to France? to work?
Are	you we they	sleeping? eating?	

Short answers

Yes, I am. / No, I'm not.

Yes, he is. / No, he isn't.
Yes, she is. / No, she isn't.
Yes, it is. / No, it isn't.

Yes, you are. / No, you aren't.
Yes, we are. / No, we aren't.
Yes, they are. / No, they aren't.

GRAMMAR

Wh- questions

What	am	I	doing?
	is	he she it	reading?
	are	we you they	

Present continuous for future

The time word shows that it's future.

I	'm am 'm not am not	meeting seeing	Maria Mrs Jones her them	tomorrow. next week. on Saturday.
He She It	's is isn't is not			
You We They	're are aren't are not			

going to future

You don't need a time word. *going to (do)* shows that it's future.

Positive and negative

I	'm am 'm not am not	going to	be	late. early.
He She It	's is isn't is not		have	a shower. dinner.
You We They	're are aren't are not		close	the door. the window.

GRAMMAR

Questions

Am	I	going to	be	late? early?
Is	he she		have	a shower? dinner?
Are	you we they		close	the door? the window?

Short answers

Yes, I am. / No, I'm not.
Yes, he is. / No, he isn't.
Yes, she is. / No, she isn't.
Yes, you are. / No, you aren't.
Yes, we are. / No, we aren't.
Yes, they are. / No, they aren't.

Wh- questions

What	am	I	going to	do? eat? buy? drink?
	is	he she it		
	are	you we they		

be: past simple tense

Positive and negative

I He She It	was wasn't was not	there. here. tired. late.
You We They	were weren't were not	

Questions

Was	I he she it	there? here? tired? late?
Were	you we they	

Short answers

Yes, I was, / No, I wasn't.
Yes, he was. / No, he wasn't.
Yes, she was. / No, she wasn't.
Yes, it was. / No, it wasn't.
Yes, you were. / No, you weren't.
Yes, we were. / No, we weren't.
Yes, they were. / No, they weren't.

Wh- questions

Where	was	I? he? she? it?
	were	you? we? they?

GRAMMAR

Have got

Positive

I / You / We / They	've / have	got	a book. an ID card. **some** pens.
He / She	's / has		

Negative

I / You / We / They	haven't / have not	got	a book. an ID card. **any** pens.
He / She	's / has		

Questions

Have	I / you / we / they	got	a book? an ID card? any pens?
Has	she / he		

Short answers

Yes, I have. / No, I haven't.
Yes, you have. / No, you haven't.
Yes, we have. / No, we haven't.
Yes, they have. / No, they haven't.
Yes, she has. / No, she hasn't.
Yes, he has. / No, he hasn't.

Wh- questions

What	have	I / you / we / they	got?
	has	he / she	

Can

Positive and negative

I / You / He / She / It / We / They	can / can't / cannot	do (it). swim. speak (French).

GRAMMAR

Questions

| Can | I
you
he
she
it
we
they | do it?
swim?
speak (French)? |

Short answers

Yes, I can. / No, I can't.
Yes, you can. / No, you can't.
Yes, he can. / No, he can't.
Yes, she can. / No, she can't.
Yes, it can. / No, it can't.
Yes, we can. / No, we can't.
Yes, they can. / No, they can't.

Wh- questions

| What | can | I
you
he
she
it
we
they | do? |

Would like

Positive and negative

| I
You
He
She
We
They | 'd
would

wouldn't | like | a cup of tea.
an apple.
some chips. |

Questions

| Would | you
he
she
they | like | a cup of tea?
an apple?
some chips? |

Short answers

Yes, please. / No, thank you.
or
Yes, I would. / No, I wouldn't.
Yes, he would. / No, she wouldn't.

Wh- questions

| What | would | you
he
she
they | like? |

GRAMMAR

Do

Present simple tense (routines)

Positive

I / You / We / They	get up / finish / start	at 7 o'clock. / at 8.30. / at 9.15.
He / She / It	starts / gets up / finishes	

Negative

I / You / We / They	don't / do not	get up / start / finish	at 7 o'clock. / at 8.30. / at 9.15.
He / She / It	does not / doesn't		

Questions

Do	I / you / we / they	get up / start / finish	at 7 o'clock? / at 8.30? / at 9.15?
Does	he / she / it		

Short answers

Yes, I do. / No, I don't.
Yes, we do. / No, we don't.
Yes, they do. / No, they don't.
Yes, you do. / No, you don't.
Yes, he does. / No, he doesn't.
Yes, she does. / No, she doesn't.

Wh- questions

What	do	I / you / we / they	do?
	does	he / she / it	

like / don't like

Positive

I / You / We / They	like	her. / jazz. / swimming.
He / She	likes	

Negative

I / You / We / They	don't / do not	like	her. / jazz. / swimming.
He / She	does not / doesn't		

Questions

Do	I / you / we / they	like	her? / jazz? / swimming?
Does	he / she		

Short answers

Yes, I do. / No, I don't.
Yes, you do. / No, you don't.
Yes, we do. / No, we don't.
Yes, they do. / No, they don't.
Yes, he does. / No, he doesn't.
Yes, she does. / No, she doesn't.

GRAMMAR

Wh- questions

What Who	do	I you we they	like?
	does	he she it	

Did

Past simple tense: irregular verbs

Positive

I You He She We They	had got bought	a ticket some tickets	yesterday. last week.

Negative

I You He She We They	didn't did not	have get buy	a ticket any tickets	yesterday. last week.

Questions

Did	I you he she we they	have get buy	a ticket? any tickets?

Short answers

Yes, I did. / No, I didn't.
Yes, you did. / No, you didn't.
Yes, he did. / No, he didn't.
Yes, she did. / No, she didn't.
Yes, we did. / No, we didn't.
Yes, they did. / No, they didn't.

Wh- questions

What	did	I you he she it we they	do?

GRAMMAR

Regular verbs

Positive

I You She He We They	stayed lived studied	there in England	last year. in 2001.

Negative

I You She He We They	didn't did not	stay live study	there in England	last year. in 2001.

Questions

Did	I you he she we they	stay live study	there? in England?

Short answers

Yes, I did. / No, I didn't.
Yes, you did. / No, you didn't.
Yes, he did. / No, he didn't.
Yes, she did. / No, she didn't.
Yes, we did. / No, we didn't.
Yes, they did. / No, they didn't.

Spelling rules

+ ed	+ d	y to -ied	double the consonant
work → worked start → started	live → lived move → moved	marry → married study → studied	stop → stopped

Contractions

am	am not	are	are not	is	is not	would	would not
'm	'm not	're	aren't	's	isn't	'd	wouldn't
cannot	have	have not	has	has not	do not	does not	did not
can't	've	haven't	's	hasn't	don't	doesn't	didn't

The Publisher and Authors would like to thank the many teachers and institutions who piloted this material in Brazil, China, Eire, France, Hungary, Italy, Mexico, Poland, Spain, and the UK.

Authors' Acknowledgements:
In a complex series like this, which has taken several years to prepare, pilot, and produce, many people are involved and have creative input. We wish to thank the many people at OUP who participated in making this book.
We would like to add our further personal thanks to Catherine Smith (Project Manager and Student's Book Editor), Richard Morris (Designer for all components), Debra Emmett (Editor 3 in 1 Practice Pack), and Madeleine Williamson (Editor, Teacher's Book and Photocopiables).

Acknowledgements:
Hello Goodbye written by John Lennon and Paul McCartney reproduced with kind permission by Northern Songs LTD/Sony ATV Music Publishing. Baby Please Don't Go words and music by Joe Williams (c) 1965 Universal/MCA Music Publishing Ltd, 77 Fulham Palace Road, London, W6. Used by permission of Music Sales Ltd. All rights reserved. International Copyright secured.

Illustrations by:
Pete Beard pp. 92/3, 178; Kate Charlesworth pp. 126/7, 157, 189/199, 202; Stephen Conlin p. 82/3; Mark Duffin pp. 38, 184, 191, 194, 201; Fran Jordan pp. 72, 91, 168, 172; Neil Gower p. 154; Tim Kahane pp. 80, 81, 129, 131, 186, 196; Sarah Nunan pp. 142/3, 188, 198; Gavin Reece pp. 44, 47, 88, 120/1, 162; Paul Sample pp. 17, 173, 180, 182, 190, 192, 200; David Semple pp. 64-66; Jonathan Williams pp. 31, 98/9, 106-8; Daniel Viney p. 160

Commissioned photography by:
Steve Betts: pp. 6, 7(tl), 9(tl), 10, 121, 13r, 18, 22, 23(tl), 23(tr), 23(br), 28/29, 30(bl), 30bc, 30(br), 30t, 30c, 32tc, 32bc, 32t, 32b, 33, 36h, 39, 40cl, 41(bl), 41(tl), 41(br), 43t, 43c, 43b, 48, 49, 50l, 50r, 51(tl), 51(bl), 51(tr), 51(br), 53(tl), 53(bl), 53(tr), 53cr, 53(br), 54/55, 57(tl), 59b, 69t, 69b, 70, 80, 91t, 91c, 91b, 155, 185(tl), 185(bl), 185(tr), 185(br), 195(tl), 195bl195(tr), 195br; Mark Mason: p. 94(br); Peter Viney: pp. 24, 40(tl), 49(tr), 76-77

The publishers would like to thank the following for their kind permission to reproduce photographs:
AKG - London p. 67 M.C. Escher's "Drawing Hands" © 2002 Cordon Art B.V. - Baarn - Holland; BBC Picture Research & Library p. 163; Bournemouth News and Picture Service p. 130 (t); Britstock-IFA p. 34 Roger Cracknell (tl), p. 57 Index Stock/Stewart Cohen (cl); BT Communication Products p. 170 (b); Camelot Group Plc p. 124 (t); Canon (UK) Ltd p. 40 (tc); Corbis UK Ltd. p. 9 Constantinos Loumakis (bl), p.12 Leif Skoogfors (r), p.14 ER Productions (bl), p.19 Fotografia, Inc. (tl), p. 34 Craig Aurness (bl), Nik Wheeler (br), p. 59 Allana Wesley White (t), p. 62 Lynn Goldsmith (l), p. 63 Jose Luis Pelaez (c), p. 84 Edward Holub, p. 85 James L. Lance, p. 86 Steve Chenn (t), Kevin R. Morris (b), p. 96 Kevin Fleming (t), p. 102 Jonathan Blair (f), Patrik Giardino (e), Wartenberg Picture Press (a), Jennie Woodcock; Reflections Photolibrary (c), p. 104 Jean-Pierre Lescourret, p. 114 Henry Diltz (tr), Robbie Jack (tb, cr), TempSport (bc), p. 116 Jim Cornfield (d, h), Jack Hollingsworth (c, g), Ken Kaminesky (b, I), Harold Miller (e, j), p.122 Elizabeth Chucker (cr), Richard Hamilton Smith (t), Paul A. Souders (bc), p. 130 Bob Krist (cl), Doug Wilson (cr), p. 132 Richard Cummins (t), p. 134 Anthony Bannister; Gallo Images (c), Layne Kennedy, p. 137 Lawrence Manning, p. 138 Jeff Albertson (tl), David H. Wells (c), p. 145 Bettmann (c), Hulton-Deutsch Collection (b), p. 147 Catherine Karnow (br), p. 165 Tim Kiusalaas, p. 166 Phil Schermeister, p. 179 Gianni Dagli Orti, p. 181 Judy Griesediek (bc), Wally McNamee (b), Gavin Wickham; Eye Ubiquitous (t), p. 183 Michael Cole (br); Dan Sinclair p. 60; Ursula Murphy, p. 146 (tr); Empics p. 42 Mike Egerton; Eurostar Group Limited p. 133; Ford Motor Company (UK) p. 41 (tl); Getty Images p. 9 FPG International (tr), The Image Bank (br), p. 14 FPG International (br), p. 19 Stone (br), p. 34 Stone (tr), p. 40 FPG International (cr), p. 62 FPG International (r), p. 63 The Image Bank (r), p. 87 The Image Bank, p. 102 Stone (d), p. 111 Stone, p. 112 The Image Bank (t), p. 114 Robbie Jack (tl), p. 115 Stone, p. 122 FPG International (br), The Image Bank (c), p. 138 Telegraph Colour Library (tr), p. 141 FPG International, p. 146 The Image Bank (bl), p. 149 The Image Bank, p. 150 The Image Bank; Hemera Technologies p. 14 (tr), p. 27, p. 36 (a-g, I), p. 40 (c), p. 41 (cr), p. 50 (c), p. 58, p. 62 (c), p. 74-75, p. 94 (a-i), p. 96 (cr), p. 114 (bl), p. 122 (bl), p. 138 (b), p. 139, p. 153 (c, r), p. 156 (c), p. 158, p. 161, p. 183 (tl, cl, bl, bc), p. 193 (tl, tc, tr, br, c); Hulton Archive p. 68, p. 109, p. 145 (t); John Birdsall p. 146 (tl); PhotoDisc p. 19 (bl, tc, tr), p. 71, p. 73, p. 89, p. 101, p. 102 (b), p. 104, p. 125; Photofusion Picture Library p. 96 Mark Campbell (br), p. 147 Paul Baldesare (tr, cr); Powerstock Superstock p. 14 (tl), p. 96 (bl); Rex Features p. 26, p. 35 Rangefinders, p. 130 Today (b), p. 134 David Hartley (b), p. 146 (cr, br), p. 147 (tl), p. 153 Phil Yeomans (l), p. 156 Nils Jorgensen, p. 159, p. 167, p. 175 Dennis Stone, p. 181 (tc); Robert Opie Collection p. 118; Ronald Grant Archive p. 40 (tr), p. 116 Pathe (a, f); Stonesfield Design p. 40 Richard Morris (b); Strathclyde Passenger Transport p. 79; Stuart Conway p. 170 (t); The British School of Motoring Ltd p. 147 (bl); Zooid Pictures p. 183 (cr, c)